Looking Down on the Moon

Poetry and Art by

Betty A. Harbison, S.S.S.

Looking Down on the Moon
© 2025 Betty A. Harbison, S.S.S.
ISBN: 978-1-966337-13-3
Library of Congress Control Number: 2025915716

Cover art: "Looking Down on the Moon"
© 2025, Betty A. Harbison, S.S.S.

Illustrations © 2025, Betty A. Harbison, S.S.S.

First Edition, 2025

Printed in the United States of America

Daxsonpublishing.com
Los Angeles, Ca
90022

Edited by Grace Beck
Cover Design by Jolene Garrettson
Layout Design by Jolene Garrettson

This volume of poetry and art is dedicated to my mother, the original, incomparably gifted and talented Betty N. Harbison, for whom by day I shadow and by night I shine. I also dedicate this book to Mabel L. Effs, Leona R. Gibbs, Miriam Ricks and all English teachers, professors and librarians dedicated to engendering and defending the love of language, literature and thought in others, especially the younger ones. Furthermore, I dedicate this book to you, dear reader, who embrace with me the soul, breath, depth, and power of words.

Epigraph

To fling my arms wide
In the face of the sun
Dance! Whirl! Whirl!
Till the quick day is done.
Rest at pale evening...
A tall, slim tree...
Night coming tenderly
    Black like me.

(from "Dream Variations" by Langston Hughes)

Looking Down on the Moon

Table of Contents

Academia

Montage of Mentors

Acknowledgments

This book came to fruition with the help of many over the course of my life, many more than the lines of poetry in any book could contain, but I would be remiss if I missed naming a few names:

to the Almighty Triune God, Who "knit me in my mother's womb" and brought and carries me in existence

to my parents, Molten A. Harbison, Jr., and Betty N. Harbison who brought me into this world, who first exposed me to honoring the world of books, culture, music, and the arts, who encouraged my explorations beyond the "best of their financial ability" and taught me to internalize, "Go!" on innumerable levels

to my publisher Erica Castro, my friend, and Daxsonpublishing, without whose unwavering confidence and timely help, this book would not exist

to my teachers and administrators, who not only offered tools to unlock the exploration but also made a way, suggested a way, or got out of the way of my exploration

to family, friends, mentors, church members, Sorors and Sisters, who have poked, prodded and harangued me for years, as well as presented me with ripped napkins, flyers, business cards, newspaper cuttings, emails, and snail mail announcements related to reading, writing, publishing and performing for the teacher and not her students. Most recently, I wish to acknowledge the following folk: my cousins Carlotta J. Fox, Marshall Fox, Lucy D. Suddreth, Dr. Cassandra "Micky" Kirkpatrick; dear friends Stephanie Gibbs, Dolores Ricks, Linda Ricks Pettis, Clarence and Elsie Dixon, Bobby and Vivian Smith, Marian Donkor, Maggy Bracamontes, Sylva Minassian, Dr. Theresa Yugar, Dr. Debora Johnson, Dr. Carolyn Lobo, Leslie Austin, Alison McDonough, Dave Crittendon, Mark and Roseana Kuczynski, Frank and Letty Zaragoza; mentors Mabel L. Effs, Gloria Lindsay, Dr. Charlotte Alston, Dr. Vernon Broussard, Dr. Mabel Hayes, Dr. Betty Bamberg, Dr. Lauri Scheyer, Dr. David Male, Doña Dolores Soto, Dr. Don Lee White, Dr. J. Harrison Wilson, Dr. Raleigh Bastien, Dr. Albert McNeil, Dr. Allan Casson; Sorors Danellen Joseph, Miriam White, Juanita McNamee, Dr. Harriette Williams, Dorothy Jackson Hayes, Tonya Richardson, Dr. Carolyn Kimble-Singleton, Dr. Gwendolyn Wyatt, Jacquelyn Snead, Mable Simon,

Barbara J. Johnson, Denise Robinson, Henrietta Elmore-Smith, Marcia Wade, Gloria Lee; to the Sisters of Social Service Los Angeles 2019/2023 Councils and Formation Teams, Sr. Deborah Lorentz, SSS, Sr. Theresa Marie Mei Chih Chen, SSS, Sr. Anne Arabome, SSS, Sr. Jennifer Gaeta, SSS, Sr. Patricia Mc Gowan, SSS, Sr. Rochelle Mitchell, SSS, Sr. Lois Marie Davis, SSS, Sr. Beatriz Tavera Guijosa, SSS, Sr. Ellen Hunter, SSS, Sr. Michele Walsh, SSS, Sr. Shaun Marie Wise, SSS, Sr. Carol Pack, SSS, Sr. Grace Boys, SSS, Sr. Martha Vega, SSS, Sr. Yolanda Vega, SSS, Sr. Catherine Connell, SSS, Sr. Beth Molmberg, SSS, Sr. Teresita Saavedra, SSS, Sr. Anne Carrabino, SSS, Sr. Diana Sabia, SSS, Sr. Sonia Delima, SSS, Sr. Annamaria Rebus, SSS, Sr. Joeline Santiago, SSS, Sr. Avigail Ortega Torres, SSS, Sr. Irma Gloria Murrieta, SSS, Sr. Leticia Tapia Espinoza, SSS, Sr. Maria Elena Salinas Santos, SSS, Sr. Isabel García Rodriguez, SSS, Sr. Marcia Sims, SSS, Sr. Vangie Lasao, SSS, Sr. Anne Field, SSS, Sr. Rachel Shepard, SSS, Sr. Marilena Narvaez, SSS, Sr. Theresa Yih-Lan Tsou, SSS, Sr. Carmela Lacayo, SSS, Sr. Albertina, Morales, SSS, Sr. Jeanne Felion, SSS, Sr. Marianna Halsmer, SSS, Sr. Claire Graham, SSS, Sr. Merita Dekat, SSS, Sr. Martha McCarthy, SSS, Sr. Eva Marie Lumas, SSS, Sr. Diane Donahue, SSS, Sr. Paula Vandegaer, SSS, Sr. Esther Lerch, SSS, Sr. Una Feeney, SSS, Sr. Sheila Walsh, SSS, Sr. Mary Josita Wilturner, SSS, Sr. Anne Lehner, SSS, Sr. Magdolna Kövári, SSS, Sr. Agnes Pataki, SSS, Sr. Marta Andrascikova, SSS, Sr. Anna Farmati, SSS, Sr. Orsloya Fecske, SSS, Sr. Suzanne Simo, SSS, Sr. Monika Kiss, SSS, Sr. Lily Teodora Danescu, SSS, Sr. Rita Vizvardy, SSS, Sr. Anna Toth, SSS, and my cohorts, Sr. Elizabeth Lopez, SSS, Sr. Raquel Cruz, SSS, and Sr. Mary Grace Nicolas, SSS; Sr. Gloria Marie Jones, OP, Sr. Glenn Anne Mc Phee, OP, Sr. Cecilia Canales, OP, Sr. Patricia Ann Smith, OP, Sr. Pauline Bouton, OP, Sr. Rebecca Shinas, OP, Sr. Isabel Espinoza, OP, Sr. Canisia Getz, OP, Sr. Mercia Zerwekh, OP; Sr. Jamie Phelps, OP, Sr. Addie Lorraine Walker, SSND, Sr. Josita Colbert, SNDdeN, Sr. Melinda Pellerin, SSJ, Sr. Anita Smith, OSF, Sr. Gayle Lwanga Crumbley, RGS, Sr. Barbara Jean La Rochester, OCD, Sr. Barbara Spears, SNJM, Sr. Nicole Trahan, FMI, Sr. Anita Baird, DHM, Sandra Coles-Bell, Sr. Limétèze Pierre-Gilles, SSND, Sr. Mary Antona Ebo, FSM, Sr. Teresita Weind, SNDdeN, Sr. Kathleen Bryant, RSC, Sr. Sara Michael King, CSJ, Sr. Sharon Becker, CSJ

to Fr. Francis Colborn, Fr. Anthony Bozeman, SSJ, Fr. Godwin Akpan, SSJ, Msgr. Richard Martini, Fr. Allan Roberts, Rev. Glenn Jones, Rev. L. Clayton Hammond, Rev. Dr. William Epps, Minister Shirlevia Jones, Fr. Bryan Massingale, Fr. Bernard Viagappan, Fr. Bill Bolton, Deacon Emile

Adams, Deacon Mark Race, Deacon James Carper, Dr. Shannen Dee Williams, Olga Sarabia, Jeanne Templeton, Vicky Lopez, Terry Staeheli, Renee Dorrance, Damaris Bradish, Maggie Gross, Monica Hughes, Mary Collins Smith, Linda Schultz, Carol James, Evelyn Payne, Elizabeth Quinn, Anita Thomas, Rochelle Romo, Frances Leon, Albert and Alnoye Haylock, Shirley Massie, Andrea Harris, Erik Jackiw, Joyce Reiley, Sandra Tufts, Pat Payne, Sue Bright, Tracy Revels, Dr. Zoia A. Smith, P. T.

to Hobart House for being a supportive sounding board—listening to and asking me to explain ideas, symbols, and illustrations

to Encino House for giving me a place and space to work on my manuscript and art during deadline crunches with time to play with their pup, Sweet Pea

to Ulloa House for granting me time for Zoom meetings and calls with book production staff during my visit

to Summit House in Buffalo, NY, for challenging me to honor body along with mind and soul

to House of Ruth staff, students, and parents (and our extended "familia") as we inspire, aspire, cheer on and cheer up one another in all aspects of "life and living"

to the wonderfully diverse, creative, supportive, and committed students, parents, faculty, and staff of Schurr High School, where I had the privilege of teaching every day for thirty-five of my thirty-eight years as a high school English teacher; and to the school "familia" at Sacred Heart High School, where I spent a three-year adventure with just the "ladies" in an openly faith-filled environment

to my fellow former Board Members of the California State University, Los Angeles Center for Contemporary Poetry and Poetics for all your generous sharing of yourselves, your gifts, your time and your resources

to Professor Hiram Sims and the Community Literature Initiative; the CLI Book Production Staff, Emily Anne Evans, Tekira Briscoe, Starr Brock; the Sims Library Staff and volunteers; the "Double # 1's," my C.L.I./ USC Chapter, Session 11 classmates—all so incredibly gifted, talented, encouraging, empowering and committed to each other's "becoming" to students, colleagues and strangers who say and have said things, such as "Is that poem in a book 'cause I'd buy it?" or "Thanks for helping me get published, Miss? When are you going to do that?" (I am "calling in these chips" eternally, beginning now... .)

to all readers/listeners—"Thank you! Thank you! THANK YOU!"
to all writers, aspiring or professional—"Write on! Write on! WRITE ON!"

Preface

My fondest hopes are that this book of poetry both affirms and reassures audiences that poetry can be about anything that touches our lives, that language offers us a means to play using many formats, levels, styles, genres, …, that words possess incredible power to generate thought and inspire action. I pray audiences will be inspired to delve into their own creative possibilities in whatever pursuits pique their fancies and to encourage and to support creative human beings around them and inside them wherever people happen to venture—at worship, work or play.

To my fellow educators, I hope you laugh, work and play along with your students as you share these poems aloud. Read to them no matter their ages. We humans are hard-wired for story-telling and audio feeds. Never forget to listen to and to learn from the great advice and wisdom you generously share with students (and they with you).

To all my fellow creatives, I finally act on the advice I often have given to students in both my classes and members of the afterschool artists and writers club, Spartans of the Plume:

> You are the only person who can create your work
> with your particular perspective. If you choose
> not to create it or not to share it, that gift remains lost
> to the universe for all eternity.

My fellow "volcanic creatives," go ahead. EXPLODE!

When asked if one of my works encapsulates this book or myself, I return to a poem I produced as a third or fourth grader, my first and practically the only one I can recite from memory, one I ponder from time to time:

> Silent is the rose
> that stands all alone.
> Be careful and quick!
> Its thorns are its throne.

B.A.H.

Nature

Deciduous

There's something to be said of winter trees
bereft of leaves, save barren nests of brown.
The ashened bark and silhouetted boughs,
revealing twiggy shapes unseen a year,
remind us quiescent limbs belie the buds
of life therein contained, dormant, waiting
for fervent kisses of the sun, bestowed
to rouse the sleeping giants from their roots
and raise the sap through veins eager to wake
from nakedness and deck in verdant robes,
so longing for each dawn 'til dusk embrace.
Gorged and sated, they explode with flow'r
and fruit and seed for bug, squirrel, bird and man
to emulate delight welcoming Lent.

It's Up to Us

Cease "talkin' loud and doin' nothin'."
Crises greet us
every day
in every way
in every newscast
Water…Weather… Food…
Water crises
Weather crises
Food crises
ultimately yield extinction for
Animals, Us, Europe, U.S., Third World, U.S., others, us…
but we can fix it.
Even with Willis' 58+ degree and climbing global warming
due to us
and melting ice caps
changing coastal landscapes and seascapes
and deoxygenated oceanic dead zones
and toxic chemical wastelands
and endangered species
due to us
and including us,
we can fix it…if we will.
Refocus Ban's Climate Enterprise triangle:
it's the government, academia, the private sector
AND all of us, especially us.

It's up to us. We know what to do
It's up to us. We know how to spread the word
It's up to us. We know how to share the knowledge and know how
It's up to us. We know how to realize creative solutions
better and faster than any generation in history
with our instantaneous communication with our neighbor
anywhere and everywhere on this orb.
It's up to us.

Fra. Elbertus knew: "We are gods in the chrysalis."
It is time to metamorphosize,

hatch out and be Barnosky's saving "force of nature"

because we can
because we must

Salvation or extinction—
for the oceans
and the rivers
and the land
and the flora
and the fauna
and all humanity...

Salvation or extinction for our world—
It's up to us.

(sources—"Mental Attitude" by Fra Elbertus; Aquarium of the Pacific lectures by Dr. Raymond Ban; Dr. Josh K. Willis and Dr. Anthony Barnosky)

Lieutenant Colonel Redwood, Retired

Strong
Straight
Solitary
Proud
Unique individual
       yet complimentary
       to the other
       "individuals" in the forest;

Among many trees—
       apart from and a part of
       mountain woods scenery before me.

Your trunk—
       so strong
       so smooth
       so prominent
so compelling—COMMANDING!

Intriguing
       without deliberate intention
       to call attention
       to itself,
       just being itself.

You continually draw me...

Why,
O Invincible, Venerable One?

I come to you
       for a closer inspection
       of your stately trunk,
           smooth—
           unlike the other redwoods
           near and far.

Nearer, I approach... nearer,
      in growing wonder
      gazing upward

Now
I see you,

"Wounded Warrior"
      stripped
      by crushing blows of living life,

but
      it is your wounds that call out to me...
      From broken branches sprout newest life!

Bark stripped never to return

but
you stand tall:
      weakness serves as witness to your dedication
      victory emanates, grafted in your vulnerability,
      a far deeper, far different strength surges
          as swift water through your sap

An imperious command to us all—
Stand up. Stand tall.
Answer life's call.

Litany of the Loss
(Endangered, Threatened or Extinct)

Too, too many of us believe
the myth of the impenetrable,
inexhaustible, mysterious element,
"the sea."
Too, too many of us like fish… cheap,
resulting in many cultures, dependent on the ocean
for their livelihood and protein,
left precariously
exploited and exploiting.
Too, too many little boats
dynamiting, poaching, and black-marketing
Too, too many big boats
bottom trawling, gill netting and by-catching
too, too much…

We are well on our way
to creating the "Sixth Extinction of the Ocean" [1]
before this century's end
with so many interdependent species and ecosystems
currently threatened or endangered
(beyond the probability
of recovery or regeneration in time):
50% of plant species gone
23% of fish species gone
70% of reptile and amphibian species gone
5% of mollusk and other species gone[2]

Too, too much waste and consumption,
whether we eat it or not—
from rockfish to codfish to haddock to halibut
to sawfish to swordfish to bacaccio to cardinalfish
to abalone to smelt to red snapper to sturgeon
to tuna to salmon to more mollusk,
to all shark but Mako to totoaba to trout
to vaquita, Chinese and Indus Rivers dolphin
to dusky sea snake to sea lion
to coral and sea grass
and too, too many species of sea turtle, whale, and seal… [3]

How soon so much, so many will be lost [4]
because of us, "the human invasion" [5]

Be wise. Get smart with the phone.
Download, then be the "APP in terra":
All People Participate
Amalgamate People Power
Attitude, Potential, Persistence
Stand in the breach between life and extinction—
no longer the human plague run rampant
but the Alliance Proactive for the Planet

Conscious, vocal
consumers bring
businesses,
fishermen,
academia
and governments
together
to "shift the paradigm"[6]
from pandemic to panacea.

Speak it!
Click it!
Be it!
Carpe diem!
#sustainability

[1] Dr. Donald Prothero: "The Sixth Extinction of the Ocean" (Aquarium of the Pacific lecture); July 9, 2015.
[2] Dr. Donald Prothero
[3] http://www.nmfs.noaa.gov/pr/species/esa/listed.htm; Dr. Donald Prothero: "The Sixth Extinction of the Ocean" (Aquarium of the Pacific lecture); July 9, 2015.
[4] Dr. Greg Stone and Christine Greene: "Trouble and Hope in an Ocean Paradise" (Aquarium of the Pacific lecture); August 20, 2015.
[5] Dr. Donald Prothero: "The Sixth Extinction of the Ocean" (Aquarium of the Pacific lecture); July 9, 2015.
[6] Chef Robert Ruiz: "Saving the Vaquita" (Aquarium of the Pacific panel discussion); August 13, 2015.

Mountains to the Sea

From the Appalachian Mountain state of West Virginia
my father came
From Beckley in Raleigh County, by way of Jumping Branch,
part of the Cherokee Nation's broken endowment,
he followed a trail,
and nothing was the same anymore

Dad followed his grandfather, who'd followed the trail
To North Carolina they came,
and nothing was the same anymore

From those same expansive mountains that respect no boundaries,
true interstate infrastructure,
true foundational sense, despite all human nonsense,
from this other state, in another small town, near another endowment,
my mother came

from Lenoir, in the shadow of Grandfather Mountain,
"the highest peak" of North Carolina's Blue Ridge Mountains
      [no matter what you read
      about their being some physiographic province
      of the Appalachians, touting Mt. Mitchell
      as the "highest point east of the Mississippi"]
In Lenoir, Dad met and married my mother,
and, two years later, I came
and nothing was the same anymore

My maternal grandmother looked out her hilltop kitchen window,
a hint of mystery in her misty eyes,
"See the Ol' Man sleeping? Look at the outline of the mountain,
child. "
I'd nod and say, "Uh-huh," before her scowl converted it to "Yes,
ma'm."
I'd nod, and try to look as mysterious and misty-eyed
as a four year old could at the mountain backdrop filling up the
window
I understand the mystery now. I still can't see him,

but I know he's there…at least his nose and forehead

Along the way, the U.S. Army shipped Dad to foreign mountains
Don't know which ones—maybe Haman, Masan, Pusan or
even the Battle of Battle Mountain—he never said much about the
Conflict
Do know that in Korean mountains
he was injured and home he came
and nothing was the same anymore

Do know we had to follow another trail
across the country for his health,
away from family, away from familiar mists and mysteries,
to a dry basin in the womb of many new mountains—

San Gabriel and San Bernadino to the north and east
Santa Ana and San Jacinto to the south and east
Santa Monica and Santa Susana to the north and west

Here, in Los Angeles, some Southern California days,
I can see 'most all these mountains,
sometimes see beyond the mountains,
sometimes see out to the sea,
with all its mists and undulating mysteries

and nothing is the same anymore…

My Baby Girl—Fourteen Years of Love

Pandora,* Pandora!
My baby girl, Pandora!
Black and white bundle
of left-pawed beauty,
curious,
Mistress of
"It's-all-about-Pandora"
—what Pandora wants to hear
—what Pandora wants to happen
until Mother passed
and cancer set in
and all the pain,
incomprehensible pain
set in,
identified late and
even more,
unidentified later

I kept telling you and your sister
to learn to speak English,
just like you understand English,
including complex sentences
You're smarter than I
(in that sense)
You understand so much more English
than I comprehend Dog.
It is what it is…

Thankfully,
we share existence
as fellow creatures.
I recognize your pain
from my pain, Mom's pain;
your misery
from my misery, Mom's misery;
your helplessness and frustration
from my care-taking frustration in helplessness,
from Mom's frustration in feeling helpless
My heart is a glass half full, half empty

from overflows that prayed you across
the divide into eternity

Your sister frolics unaffected,
even though I saw her whisper her goodbyes
in your almost deaf ears the night before
(She stays right under me.)
I've echoed this lived history, as well—
your sister's crusted over surface,
ice flow versus lava…
No question which will dominate.
Frost,** recited
in childhood classrooms,
teaches us
long before
most teachers understand
scrupulous watching,
supportive waiting,
speculative worriment
suspended on scales
between volatility and requiescence
until…

* Pandora, a German Shepherd/Malamute mix that the poet raised,
along with her sister, Penelope, Pandora's litter mate, from age ten
weeks until Jesus called Pandora home from cancer overnight between
Sunday night, October 2nd and pre-dawn Monday, October 3rd, 2022

**reference to Robert Frost's poem, "Fire and Ice"

The New Year (a Fall Impression)

Walking through a campus forest
autumn-blazed red, gold, and brown;
Winter whispers through the treetops,
bidding branches cast leaves down.

Nature works her season magic
undisturbed by beast or God.
Only man has left a marring
crowning ash with "Pepsi" pod.

Remnants of My Favorite Battleground

As I march across the battlefield of yesterday,
how tranquil seems the air

No longer are there bursts of cold white cannon balls,
spraying the atmosphere with crystal wet dust.

No longer are there piercing war cries
        from youths releasing socialized aggression

No longer is there a single spot
of ground in nature's blanket
        chaste of mankind's touch.

No fallen warriors lie cold
No enemies lie in the brush
I cross the spot carefree

All that remains are crystal
dusted patches, iced over
boot tracks, muddy winter slosh
and, here and there,
scattered balls
of ammunition—
the only remnants of my favorite
battleground now mocked
and melted by enemy Captain Sun.

But wait, four star clouds
        have rushed him.
They struggle in the East until
        darkness flanks

I, a simple soldier, wonder
        without question, the outcome

Alas, two quiet gray sky days
of coldness pass.

Then, at night, it begins—
Nature's purging blanket of white,
covering all old wartime remnants
erasing all errors of man
while he sleeps (so it seems).

We soldiers will awaken to
see glaciated supplies
captured in the East
and delivered by generals

Rounded cold white weapons will be made
War cries will resound
Attacks will commence; retreats will follow
Wounded will fall and rise quickly under fire

Many will run—
        some will laugh
        none will cry

What fun! What fun!
What fun these battles
that last less than one day!

And again, I...I will be marching
slowly across my favorite battleground
of yesterday—
        full of remnants,
        full of memories.

Zen Raking

or

" 'Do What You Can Do in the Time that You Have' * Available"

Raking is not a task that can be completed.
Raking is not a race nor a competition
with myself or another.
Raking is not to impress others.
Raking is not a senseless activity
for the sake of activity.

Raking is a joyful, sensory exercise.
Raking is a meaning-filled stewardship act
for the earth.
Raking is a source of communal and individual pride.
Raking is an act of immediate gratification or frustration.
Raking is a reminder
of finite human limitations
and infinite ramifications.

Raking is an expression of Love
for those we will never meet
ofttimes manifested for those
held deeply in our hearts.

*Quote from Sr. Patricia Marie Walsh, O.P.

Fun and Music

"After the Beep" for the Harbison Family

Illustrious soul—
To share your fame,
please remember to leave your name!

A phone number and message make it better.
If all else fails, write us a letter!

Buzz Off

I loathe you, winged worm-maker,
destroyer of every bit of matter
irritation at every celebration
ruination of hours', weeks', months' labor
born of love or obligation
when you rest,
when you touch,
when you taste
anything and everything
never asking
indiscriminately interrupting conversations
irritating all with your obnoxious noises
in our face
invading our ears
ignoring our violent waves,
audaciously mating before us
Go look for carrion.
Go away.
Buzz off!

Carol of Professor Hiram Sims'
Community Literature Initiative Class
(after the Christmas carol, "Yuletide Is Here")

C		L		I		Class	
C	L	I	Class	C	L	I	Class
C L-I	Class	C L-I	Class	C L-I	Class	C L-I	Class

"Read ev'ry day.   Write ev'ry day."   is Pro-fes-sor Hi-ram's mantra.
If you don't turn enough pa-ges in, Prof. Sims will sure-ly haunt 'cha!

(Repeat)
"Read ev'ry day.   Write ev'ry day."   is Pro-fes-sor Hi-ram's mantra.
If you don't turn enough pa-ges in, Prof. Sims will sure-ly haunt 'cha!

"Read ev'ry day!   Write ev'ry day!"
Prof. Hiram's voice   won't go away.

    Drummed in your head   at ev'ry class
    Partners text it   first day to last

Ex-per-i-ment   try some-thing new
Class-time get ten   min-utes plus two

    Even if your   poem is a mess
    work-shop-ping it   makes it a "best"

Show up, show out   for ev'ry-one!
Show up for you!   Come have some fun!

    T.A.'s bring snacks,   good and de-lish
    Save some for Prof.   That is his wish.

Four hours no break— That's nor-mal-cy… .

Park where you can   close as can be

We don't get out   e-ver ear-ly
What can you say.   It's fam-i-ly!

"Read ev'ry day!   Write ev'ry day!"
Prof. Hiram's voice   won't go away.

In-spired by class-   mates' strug-gles, too,
you'll be a-mazed   what we all do

Pub-lish your poems!   Pub-lish your book!
We guar-an-tee   you'll find your nook

Folks just like you   who made it through
present in class.   Authors at last!

Com-mun-i-ty   Lit-er-a-ture

     I-ni-tia-tive!   That is for sure.

Com-mun-i-ty   Lit-er-a-ture

     I-ni-tia-tive!   That is for sure.

Com-mun-i-ty

     Lit-er-a-ture

In-i-tia-tive!

     That is for sure.

C	L	I	Class	C	L	I	Class
C		L		I			

*Contact poet for musical transcription options or choral reading options.

Children of the Living God

(dedicated to National Association of Negro Musicians, Inc.— Georgia Laster Branch's "Spotlight on Youth")

If anybody ask you
who I am, who I am, who I am
If anybody ask you
who I am,
tell 'em I'm a child of God [1]

Greetings and welcome,
fellow children of the living God—
      endowed by our Creator
      gifted by our Heavenly Father
      graced by our beloved Holy Spirit
      blessed by our redeeming Savior, the First-born Son

Welcome, my brother! Welcome, my sister!
You are a child of the Almighty,
Brother and Sister of the King of Kings!
God has made (you)
a little lower than the angels
and has crowned (you)
with glory and honor. [2]

Never forget "who you are"
nor "Whose you are" [3]
Never forget Whose reflection you are…
"You are because God is" [4]
Be all that you are called to be…
      Gift us
      Grace us
      Bless us
      as we bless one another
      with a spirit of welcome,
      as fellow children of the living God

O child of promise—

Go bravely, go boldly
for you are never alone
even in perceived loneliness
You are surrounded
and buoyed up
by divine interconnectedness
to every other child of the living God
throughout time in memoriam—
yesterday, today and forever
      Blessed be the tie that binds...[5]
Remember your unity,
Remember your interdependence
Seek out your family
Support and be supported
by that divine energy,
child of the living God

Let the Spirit guide you
in your quest to be
all that you are called to be
It is your inheritance,
both a promise and a gift
from our Eldest Brother

The promise is not
to be free of trials and tribulations,
but the promise is to be free...
to be free to be
Give all strifes and stresses
back to God,
Who transforms them
into a blessing
for our family

Let the Spirit lead you
to fellowship with children of the light
of Christ everywhere—
from mentors to managers
from colleagues to employees

from friends to life partners

Let the Spirit deliver you
  from children of the night
  because they're out there, too,
  those who dwell in darkness,[6]
  who seek to extinguish every light

Don't "dwell in darkness"
Get back to the light
Invite others to come with you,
but get back to the light
Flee those who "dwell,"
and get back to the light

Let the Spirit of Love and Life lead you
Pursue Her and be blessed,
O child of the Eternal Light

    If anybody ask you,
  "What's yo' name, what's yo' name, what's yo' name?"
    If someone stop and ask you,
     "What's yo' name?,"
    tell 'em you're a child of God.

    Tell 'em you're a child of God
     Tell 'em everywhere
     Tell 'em, O child!

    'Cause if anybody ask you
     who I am,
     you tell 'em
    I'm a child of God [1]

[1] "Child of God," Traditional Negro Spiritual (Sing the lines.)
[2] Psalm 8:5
[3] Afro-American cultural religious expression
[4] Afro-American cultural religious expression
[5] "Blessed Be the Tie that Binds" hymn,
words and music by Richard K. and Donald S. Avery (Sing the lines.)
[6] Psalm 143:3

Creature's Last Intrusion
(In Memoriam)

T'was only grace the neighbors "nosed"—
      my schoolmates living very near!
T'was only grace I did not smite
      that dreaded creature then and there!

How I do hate brother's pitbull—
      the monster mouth with spotted hair!
I hate it claims the fam'ly's house,
      thinks where it flops its current lair!

It loped into my sacred space,
      sniffed out my belovéd Care Bear—
Strawberry patches, slobbed-on wads,
      pink tufts of fluff strewn ev'rywhere!

Oh, this time, it has crossed the line!
      Iced vengeance is the thing I dare.
If kin or monster, taint my room,
      sharp pain, slow death 'tis planned! Beware!

Epitaph for Betty A. Harbison, Child of God

Here lies one of the talented and gifted
who spent her life seeing others were lifted
Mattered not your status, religion, or race
What entered her heart, stirred her soul, held your place—
your innate quality, character, and thought
freely given by God though graces unbought

Epitaph for the Scoundrel

Here lies our scandalous preacher
who fancied himself a marvelous teacher
but revealed himself as a monstrous creature
who assaulted any female if he could reach her

Fanfare for Four
(Piano, Guitar, Trombones and Drum; SSAA)

Ta da da, Ta da da, Ta da da, Ta da da,   Tum Ta
Ta da da, Ta da da, Ta da da, Ta da da,   Tum ta ta
Ta da da, Ta da da, Ta da da, Ta da da,   Tum Ta
(pause) Ta da da, Ta da da, Ta da da, Ta da   Tum ta

Tahhhhhh-ummm   ta   ta
Tahhhhhh-ummm   ta ta   ta ta
Tahhhhhh-ummm   ta-ta-ta   ta-ta-ta
Tahhhhhh-ummm

Tum ta--

Ta da da, Ta da da, Ta da da, Ta da da,   Tum Ta
Ta da da, Ta da da, Ta da da, Ta da da,   Tum ta ta
Ta da da, Ta da da, Ta da da, Ta da da,   Tum Ta
(pause) Ta da da, Ta da da, Ta da da, Ta da   Tum ta

Tahhhhhh-ummm   ta-ta-ta, ta-ta-ta
Tahhhhhh-ummm   ta-ta-ta, ta-ta-ta
Tahhhhhh-ummmmmmmmmmmm

Schlooooooooooooooom—

                                weh
                           wee,
                     doo,
                dah,
            dah,
        dah,
     dah,
dah,

                Whaaaaaaaaaaaaaaaaaaaaaaaah!

(Yeah!)

HAIKU

Athena

Brilliant, "gray-eyed" one!
Thinker-warrior for what's right!
Fiercely creative...

Haiku Explosion

Lava can't be stopped
Seventeen syllable flow
It burns 'til it cools

Outside and In

Ooooh, this heat feels good!
Didn't know that I was cold...
God's warm sunshine kiss!

Truism

Live your life as prayer
100% won't be...
We all fail sometime

Measures

This never-ending song will one day end
its final refrain—sonorous and clarion—
after wafting through minors of blue
and modulating to exuberant heights
enough to throb the neck veins of the Met's best coloratura
in homage to Kathleen Battle
and plunging to the center of earth's basso profundo flow
in reverberations of Paul Robeson
My Majors are bliss,
accelerating by staccato and prestissimo thirds
and the beauty of fifths
and unresolved arpeggios vivace
holding a seventh with a fermata,
resolved or not
Sometimes I sing it pianissimo
Sometimes I sing it fortissimo
but the refrain…
the circle and cycle back to the refrain—
      comforting a listener with anticipatory expectation
      of what is thought to be known,
      challenging the singer to bring a new self,
          known, unknowing, no-ing and knowing
that each verse draws nearer the last and leads back here
until this never-ending song one day will end
with staggered breath exhaled in eternity.

Mix Up?!

'Twas a somber night that day
in the wintry month of May.

I stood lying in the snow
wondering where on earth to go.

Suddenly, a thought spoke out to me,
"Never print this as poetry!!!"

SQUAWK

Shrilling "Chirp! Chirp! Chirp, chirp, chirp, chirp, chirp!
Chirp! Chirp, chirp, chirp, chirp, chirp! Chirp! Chirp!
CHIRP (choke)… CHIR (cough), CHIRP, CHIR, chirrrrrp…
chirrrrrrp," chirps
fill the henhouse.

Trilling "coo, coo-coo, coo, coo-coo, coo, coo-coo-coo-coo-coo-coo-
coo,
coo, coo-coo, coo, coo-coo, coo, coo-coo-coo-coo-coo-coo-coo,
coo, coo-coo, coo-coo-coo-coo-coo-coo-coo," coos
balk sulking barnyard waddlers.

"Caw, caw, Caw, caw, caw, caw, CAW,
Caw, Caw, CAW, CAW, CAW, CAW, Caw, Caw,
Caw, Caw, CAW, CAW, CAW, CAW, Caw, caw" cawing
screeches the wandering gaggle lakeside—

Their strange yet familiar cacophony
reaches shadowed flutterers in high branches,
awakening waves of echoed
"quack, quack, quack, quack, quack,"
"quack, Quack, quack, Quack, quack …Quack, Quack, Quack…
"quack, Quack, quack, Quack, quack, Quack, Quack…"
and "Quack, Quack, Quack, Quack," quacking,
culminating with two silencing solo QUACKS!

Now ceased, their neighbors' covered
"honk…honk…honk-honk," honkings
rise from several lower branched nesting pairs,
no longer resting but still nuzzling, slightly puzzling,
as they shutter, first shocked, then stutter
into newfound strident chanting from soft
"honk-honk…honk-honk…honk-honk" and
"Honk-honk…Honk-honk…Honk-honk" to
"HONK-honk, HONK-honk, HONK-honk" climaxing
with "HONK-HONK, HONK-HONK, HONK-HONK" HONKS!

Hovering high and gawking, squawks a Red-tailed hawk,

"Cock-a-doodle dooooooo!"
His mate, cresting, dives, swishes by, then circles, jesting:

"Ain't this a HoooOOOOOOoooT?"

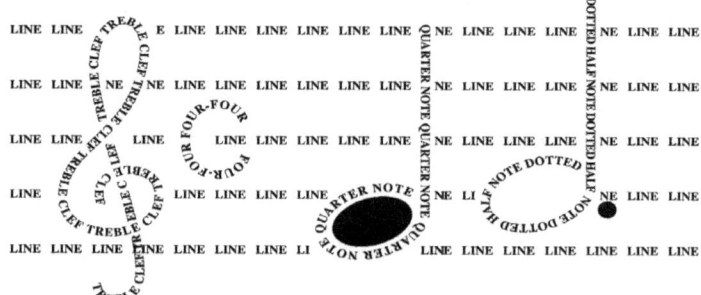

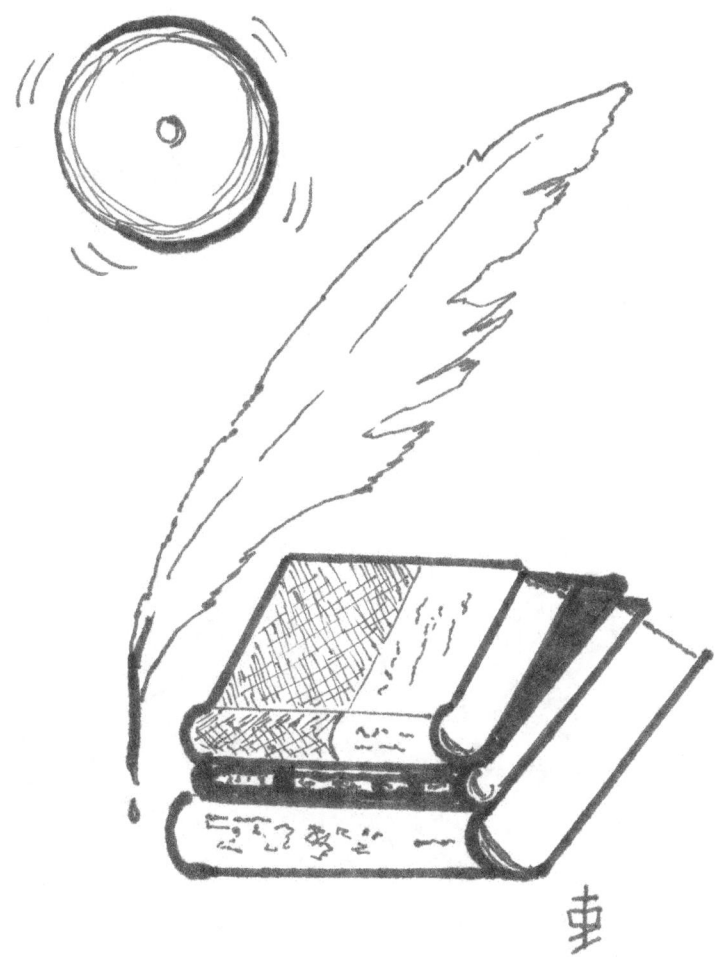

Academia

9:05 a.m.

"Clear your desks of all books and papers.
        All you need is a pen. No white-out!"
The teacher's voice booms so loudly
        against our fitful quiet
        that the window pane rattles.
He closes the door to keep out sound
        in a noiseless hall.
(Too bad it does not damper the din
        thundering in my brain
        with lightening flashes
        giving me glimmers of insight
        that blind and vanish
        as I read through only...
        three questions?!!)

CHLUNK!

Fifteen minutes of the two hours gone,
sounds the senseless, breathless,
stone cold disk mooning on the wall.

CHLUNK!

Groaning and jumping, strikingly ticking off
much, much too much

CHLUNK!

much more than moments in time

CHLUNK!

not seconds, not minutes
but lives and futures
I might be intrigued if I had...

CHLUNK!

My pen jumpstarts into mindless motion.

CHLUNK!

At 10:30 a.m., my shattered brain begins to coalesce.

CHLUNK!

My fingers barely manage notating the steady stream of brain
  dictation—
        barely legible scrawling
        barely finished scribbling
        pleads its end
        under a relentless contradiction
        of edited condensations

CHLUNK!

"Pens down. Thank you, ladies and gentlemen.
        I'll know what you think
        when I see what you say."

I exit in a blanched and blank disquietude,
        in a noisy solitude
        of silent screams.

CAASPP*

CAASPP is a pain in the asp
if anyone askps
how much it exasp-
erates young and old to the lastp
days of schooling are pastp
Until then, work hard with your classp
Yes, with each lad and lassp,
so they won't be aghastp
but garner scores that will passp
Ultimately, teachers, this is our taskp
No, can't escape with a queen's asp
Just amass points that are vastp,
then, retire and baskp
Seize whatever life is left with a firm clasp
until we breathe out a last rasp.

*The California Assessment of Student Performance and Progress, a
state-wide testing tool

Gourmet School Lunch

Peanut butter, raisins,
Cranberry "Craisins,"
Drizzled with honey,
Cinnamon, and cloves.

Triangles of brown bread
Sport seed kernels here and there.
Box of apple nectar
Drains with short, squiggly straw.

Munch, munch. Umm!
(Sweetness)
Munch, munch. Umm!
(Fragrance)
Munch, munch. Umm!

Tongue sweep.

Crumbs gone!

I Concur, Mr. Frost— "Nothing Gold Can Stay"

I love early morn
because nature is at its
summit of beauty.

Pinnacle of morn—
Diamond burst awakes the world
First light, sunrise, day!

Light reveals the "real"
beauty, ugly from the past
remnants of the dark

Hope 'gainst hope renews
One chance more to stone giants
Purpose sees us through

Hope 'gainst hope renews
One more chance to strive again
Purpose, praise the dawn…

It's So Easy, Mr. Hughes
(a response to Langston Hughes' "Harlem (2)/
What happens to a dream deferred/"or "Dream Deferred")

It's so easy to die
    when you don't know
        what it means to live

It's so easy to hate
    when you don't know
        what it means to love

It's so easy to laugh
    when you don't know
        what it means to cry

It's so easy to destroy
    when you don't know
        what it means to build

It's so easy to take
    when you don't know
        what it means to give

It's so easy to disrespect
    when you don't know
        what it means to self-respect

The answer to your question, Mr. Hughes, is so painfully easy:
        a dream deferred too long
        hides in nitroglycerine despair
        until, with agitation sufficient,
        it self-destructs
        Ka-boom!

It's so easy to kill and be killed
    when you don't know
        what it means to live and to be alive

It is far better to have had and lost*
than to have known
and never had at all

* from "In Memoriam A.H.H. 1849" by Alfred Lord Tennyson

Poetics

I love that poem because it speaks to me
although I'd be hard pressed to tell you why
Perhaps, the poet's diction is the thing
that caught my eye, but, then again, I think
it is the sound—the rhythm and the rhyme
that transports me beyond my finite self,
connecting to all beings great and small,
connected to the now, the past, the when,
beyond the finite globe on which we live
into the infinites of time and light,
eternity beyond eternity
What more can humans say about such art,
except to prattle in such epithets
that flatter innocents and fools alike,
but shame the Bard* and risk wrath from above
Invibe, inhale, infuse in deepest silence
Receive the gift and giver with delight
and deepest gratitude express in quiet

* "The Bard" refers to William Shakespeare

"What's in a name?"* Everythang!

A rose could not begin to smell as sweet
so doused in dung and other things that reek
It's why in every corner of the earth
vulgarities and epithets give birth
to degradatious slander fueling hate
From sticks, stones, knives to guns—wars escalate

Today to call one, "villain," might amuse
and guarantee sound bites and social "views,"
but call a mom by something with an udder,
her children's kicks and bites will make you shudder
Why "What up, dog?" I disallowed in class;
the implications to the mothers crass

Just watch the shyest lamb become a lion
without regard for teeth or limb or dying
at utterance of any foul phrase
the heart or honor his kinswoman slays

And how defeated peoples have become
beleaguered with arrows and slings of some
determined to oppress, malign, defame,...
How can you dare to ask, "What's in a name?"

Across the globe your works fill stage and screen
Your insight into human nature keen
I've relished teaching teens to love your works,
to delve below the surface, find what lurks
in minds of characters both young and old,
to glean life wisdom from your scenes-- pure gold
Yes, I and students love the repartee
as players quip in fun or pre-melee
A queen calls Richard "poisonous bunched-back toad."
For fourteen lines "hellhound" and "cur" explode
'pare "whoreson obscene," "-tallow-catch" to "ape."
Name-calling in your plays, there's no escape
Both snob and baseborn use much worse than this
bewitching fans who pay for tongues that hiss

The question that you pose is so absurd!
Bard, PLEASE, you know the power of a word
to tip the scales in favor or inflame.
Everythang! That's what is in a name.

* *Romeo and Juliet* by William Shakespeare

Montage of Mentors

American Juliet Sings of Her British Gentleman,

a Cambridge Professor
"Too early seen unknown, and known too late."*

It does not matter whether I am there
or whether he is here. He opens eyes.
He opens minds. I see him ev'rywhere!
He opened up my heart—foolish and wise
How can it be that I love him so much?
His eyes are blue when they should be dark brown!
His hair—gray white, his body—frail, his touch
I've never known! How can he bear my crown?
His shoulders—hunched, his smile—sweetly awry,
His brow—much knitted, face—so deeply lined…
I'm half his age! This "pensioner" most spry…
How then is he "epitome" refined?
Yet, no man else has made my light so shine
as this dear man, the first true love of mine.

* Shakespeare, Romeo and Juliet

Dare to Be a "Dr. Don Lee"[1]

Love what you do
Do what you love
Perfect your art
Study until you find pleasure and treasure in the discovery
Study until you discover your own art within your art
Study until you glimpse the infinite in the finite,
                  until you grasp your finite in infinity
Study until excellence seeks you and embraces you
              as both an ally and a friend
Study until…
              and

Share your knowledge with the world—
        Collaborate with colleagues
        Palaver with people, real people
        Herald heritage to the generations
        They are your "heirs apparent"

Know both young and old are watching you
learning from you
        emulating you
            taking pride in you
(and taking pride in themselves vicariously through you)

Demand the best from yourself;
expect no less from others
Let a tireless faith and a lifetime of work
form the prism of your eye,
that unmistakable perception
revealing seeds of excellence
        growing
beneath the rocky ground
and unplowed soil
in the human soul
Liberate the seeds!
Aerate the land
and pull the weeds of fear!

He knew his "call out's"[2] served
as stimulus and fertilizer
        for the heirs apparent
See his seedlings blossom,
reach fruition, and
        produce "good seed"
for yet another harvest of excellence—
a harvest spanning all genders and generations

Who next will farm the land?
Who next will tend the seed?
Are new laborers truly so few?

Heirs apparent,
can you hear another "call out"[2]—
one sent directly,
        unmistakably to you?

Dare, you heirs apparent!

Dare to do all you can do!

Dare to see beyond the moment,
        beyond this millennium!

Dare to move beyond the "you,"
        yet through the "you,"

Dare to pursue excellence,
        to beget excellence and
        to expect (meaning, "to accept")
        no less than excellence!

Dare to be a bulwark!
        Dare to be a blessing!
                Dare to be...
                        to be a Dr. Don Lee!

[1] Dr. Don Lee White—composer, organist, California State University Los Angeles professor 27 years, director, chorale founder, mentor, hymnologist, refined African American Christian gentleman, passed September 16, 2010

[2] A "call out" is a public singling out of an individual, verbally and/or by signal, to perform a task at that very moment; in Dr. White's case, the subject of the "call out" was given no option to decline performing the task whether or not spectators were present, and the experience usually resulted in the individual's discovery of an unknown capability or state of readiness to meet a challenge.

Epistle to Dr. J. Harrison Wilson

Dear Dr. J. Harrison Wilson,

Thank you for always living up to your reputation
for "the pursuit of excellence"
and for demanding
all around you to live
up to your expectation
for excellence.
When I heard you extol
the brilliance and beauty of Negro Spirituals
for the very first time,
then exhort audiences,
choirs and soloists to sing
with renewed pride
and unwavering commitment
to our heritage,
especially our musical heritage,
I was overjoyed
to hear a "man after my own heart!"
I was in my twenties,
fresh out of a majority university,
starting my teaching career,
and "busy"—
but, to myself,
I vowed to "make it"
to N.A.N.M. programs.

Thank you for never ceasing to invite
me to join N.A.N.M.
whenever I helped
you prepare programs in foyers
and we, well, you talked and I listened,
especially before I learned
no one ever has time.
We have to
"take it to make it."

I will always admire, respect and remember you fondly.

Love,

Betty A.
one of your many legacies

p.s.
Your memorial once again set the standard—
MUSIC, MUSIC, and more MUSIC!
I am not giving anyone permission
to talk at mine, either.

p.p.s.
By the way, I joined N.A.N.M. and the Symphonic Chorale.

B.A.H.

Epistle to My Mother

Dear Mother,

Thank you for exposing me, from infancy,
       to our heritage in music—the Negro Spiritual!
Thank you for passing on the musical genes
       and expectations of the descendants of Henry T.
Thank you for making sure that Dad purchased a piano
       when we moved to California,
              long before we could envision buying a house here.
Thank you for playing all those Earl Garner records.
       By the way, Dad blasted Ray Charles albums
          when you weren't at home.
          (Yeah, I know. You knew.)
Thank you for practicing Chopin, Debussy, Rachmaninoff and
  Dett's "Juba Dance" for hours.
Thank you for forcing me to take music lessons all those years
       and for waking me up at 5:30 a.m. on Sunday mornings
       to listen to the Morman Tabernacle Choir before dressing
      for church.
Thank you for getting me into the Adult Choir to sing with you
       at Christ Community United Methodist Church
          when I was an eighth grader.
Thank you for arranging music dinners with the Dunlaps,
       where I sang and you accompanied,
          following our "printed program."
Thank you for all the years and all the places
       you have accompanied me.
Thank you for encouraging me to take voice lessons.
Thank you for critiquing my performances
       in every field—music, drama, poetry or prose.
(You are the only person I know who can recount audience
  reaction
       from every side, *including several rows behind you.*)
Thank you for dragging me all over California
       and portions of the Southeast
          to experience, oh, so many things…together.
Thank you for letting me drag you all over the world
       to share, oh, so many things…together.

I'm so glad that God gave you to me, Mother.
Without you,
I never would have considered nor conceived
sharing my art, my poetry and my voice
simultaneously
with an audience
of musicians.

"There is no other like my mother."

Much love and many blessings,

"Your one and only" Songbird

p.s.
Maybe, I will re-approach the piano, *someday.*
Oddly enough, I enjoyed playing at Bennett College
freshman year, except for "Juries."
St. Monica prayed for St. Augustine's conversion for thirty years.
Never give up. From mothers spring hope eternal.
B.A.H.

Epistle to the National Association of Negro Musicians, Inc. and the Georgia Laster Branch*

Beloved N.A.N.M., Beloved G.L.B.*!

Thank you for believing me a *musician*
long before I attached the word as a self-descriptor.

I called myself a sassy, second soprano,
—sometimes "on loan" to the firsts,
—sometimes "clowning around" with the second altos or basses,
        a choir singer.
I only considered voice lessons as a young adult
to sing better to God's glory "in da chwyr."

"Thank you" to Voice Teacher-Member Sarah Mc Ferrin,
who kept talking
about "when you sing solos"…
        I smiled to myself with an invisible eye roll,
        but eventually I did… .

"Thank you" to Voice Teacher-Member Gwendolyn Wyatt,
who kept talking
about "when you sing solos with instrumental ensembles…,"
        I laughed loudly to myself with internal head-shaking,
        but eventually, I did…
        as a founding member of the Gwen Wyatt Community Chorale**

I like who I am around N.A.N.M. musicians.
        I like who I become around you.

I joined the Symphonic Chorale as an affirmation to an invitation
from the late G.L.B. President J. Harrison Wilson.

"Thank you," Founder/Director-Member Dorothy Jackson Hayes,
because you listen,
really listen, to your choir of musicians—
chorally, individually, one-on-one,…
You took me under your "Mother's wing"
gave me solos and duets

expected "sight-singing,"
(I am so much better than I was when I started.)
affirmed my musicianship
called me, "musician," in your choir of musicians
(and I believed you.)

I like who I am around N.A.N.M. musicians.
        I like who I become around you.

I joined the Delta Choraliers while still an undergrad at 'S.C.***

"Thank you," Founder/Director-Member Danellen Joseph,
who warmly welcomed
this college junior among the "real" adults
You modeled showmanship and stage presence for me
taught me to how to "play with" and "enjoy" the audience
set me free onstage
set me free to explore all my artistic avocations
supported me in supporting others—young and old—
in performance, in all the arts
Subconsciously and consciously,
I see you,
I hear you,
I emulate you.

I like who I am around N.A.N.M. musicians.
        I like who I become around you.

"Thank you" to N.A.N.M. National Conventions,
where the push and pull of excellence
begets excellence
        and begets more excellence,
which begets more dreams of excellence for us all—
young and old,
advocate and expert
amateur and professional
Behold in finite gathering space a micro-universe of human resources
for our music history and mystery in America—

I like who I am around N.A.N.M. musicians.
    I like who *I've become* around you.

I am a true disciple—*one who is always learning*
I can access "spoken music" in my head,
can have it written down—
        transcribed for the world to hear,
                for the world to perform
I can point others, others who look like me,
in the right direction
        to be nourished
in pursuit of their dreams
in pursuit of their excellence—our aggregate excellence!

I like who I am around N.A.N.M. musicians.
    I like who I've become around you—
            always a writer
            always a poet
            also an artist
            now a musician.

May God continue to "bless the work of your hands," especially with our youth.

                    Love,

                    Betty A.

p.s.
Never forget to keep inviting folks to join
again and again, year after year.
They will like who they become *around you.*

                    B.A.H.

* now the Georgia Laster Association of Musicians, Inc. (G.L.A.M., Inc.)
**now the Gwen Wyatt Chorale
***University of Southern California

Keeper of the Keys

(dedicated to Rev. Janesia Fuller-Mosley,
Youth Director, National Association of Negro Musicians, Inc.)

Our pearls of great price

    we entrust to you

    —the ones for whom
    we must give
    all we have
    to keep them secure

We trust you to keep them
    safe and sound

    —the ones for whom
    we must sacrifice
    all we have
    as investment
    for the future

We know that you will keep them
    safe and sound

    —even from ourselves
    who might exploit them
    before they have reached
    their full potential

When you bring them out
    for us to see,
        we find their beauty
        and exuberance
        irresistible

We want to sound them
                test them
                rate them
                compare them
                show them
                share them

        with the world
        and ourselves
        all at once

but because we love them
and cherish them,

we entrust them to you—
        the Keeper of the Keys

We know that you will keep them
        safe and sound

How we long to sound and savor them
        in the apex of their youth!

We so believe in them
        as we behold them
        in and out of world's season

We see them as only we can—
our own images reflected
from eternity to eternity…

Keeper of the Keys
through your deliberate action
        you help us, in our sheer delight,
        not to deplete their energies,
        but to enhance their resources
        you remind everyone
        not to depreciate their intrinsic value for an instance of glory
        but to assure that they ascend the heights of excellence
        (in due time)

Keeper of the Keys
under the gaze of your jurisdiction,
        unanimously given
                because we trust you to keep them
                        safe and sound,
we polish...

        we polish with well-preserved cloths of silken hopes,
        woven by named and nameless generations,
        even beyond our conscious collective's reckoning,

        we polish with oil squeezed drop by drop from many lives' work
                canvassed end to end from the dawn of human history
                        in the twinkle of God's eye

        we polish and polish and polish
                with elaborate community effort

and we wait...

        anxious for the effervescence
        our hearts palpate through our fingertips

Keeper of the Keys
because we trust you to keep them safe and sound,
you help us
        not to over-do nor under-do

you balance the scales
        between epitaph and epitome

Chosen sentinel for our youth!
Faithful guardian of their genius!
We salute you—
We applaud you—
Our Keeper of the Keys!

Sr. Anne Lehner—
She Shall Teach Me How to Live Again and Again

She taught me how to live;
she shall teach me how to live again and again…

She, who heard the call of love
over a score and half century ago,

She, who endured all manner of tribulation—
college air raids, novitiate army invasions,
communist harassment, religious persecution,
companions shot and imprisoned,
illegal immigration, constant surveillance
and blacklisting to guarantee
joblessness, homelessness and starvation,
she trusted "God is good…all the time"
(often through the rendering hands of strangers,
intransigently embracing the perils of love
on behalf of foreigners in foreign lands)

She, whose Beloved transformed
what appeared to be
"exile" with Sr. Margaret* from the European underground
into re-emergence "above ground,"
with expansion far beyond the envisioned west**

She taught me how to live;
she still teaches me how to live again and again…

She, who strove to radiate solely love of her Beloved,
imparted peace from His peace,
comfort from His comfort,
joy from His joy
and wisdom from His wisdom.

She taught me how to live;
she teaches me how to live again and again and again…

What she received from the love of her Beloved,

she held with working, open hands and a keen ever-working mind,
seeking any and many and more opportunities
to share her love for a sister or a brother
always with His grace
always with her gratitude—
gratitude expressed to you,
gratitude expressed to me;
kindness shown to you,
kindness shown to me;
prayer poured out for you,
prayer poured out for me

born of an intimacy and an honesty and an abandonment
and a freedom and a surrender;
born of a communion, now a consummate union with her Beloved
beyond all aging, all aching, all suffering,
beyond all perceived limitations.

"The most important thing is love. That's the most important thing."
crossed her lips more than once.

She taught me by living her life in the light of love and truth,
and she shall ever teach me
by her gallant, grace-filled leap into His loving Arms

*Sr, Margaret Slachta, Foundress of the Society of the Sisters of Social Service in Hungary

**originally the United States East Coast in Buffalo, New York, but later expanded to the West Coast in Los Angeles, California

Sr. Margaret's Sail

And...darkness was upon the face of the deep.
And the Spirit of God moved upon the face of the waters.[1]

Following the footsteps of our foundress, Sr. Margaret,[2]
Sisters of Social Service set sail
with the Spirit of God, moving upon the face of the waters

We sail on,
navigating by prayer and listening
to the Spirit of God, moving upon the waters

We sail on
into uncharted waters,
waters uncharted in Adam's worldly experience,
waters uncharted in "man's inhumanity to man,"
but envisioned by prophets and imagined by children,
fought for and brought to moments of fruition
in many cultures and many places and many struggles
through the grace of the Spirit of God,
calling all Her children to move upon the face of the waters.

Our course is set and re-set,
adjusted together,
as we listen, we establish, we empower, and we sail on

We, Sisters of Social Service, sail on
with the Spirit of God, moving upon the face of the waters

We, Sisters of Social Service, workers for social good and goodly service,
   sail on
resolved to dissolve
conditions that oppress
                and
systems that regress

We, Sisters of Social Service, workers for social good and goodly service,

  sail on
committed to combat
tyrants that digest
                and
officials that digress
to impress the corrupted
at the expense of the progress
of God's people and God's world

To sail on, we listen, we establish, we empower, we move
through our "diversities of gifts"[3]
and our "differences of ministries"
and our "diversities of activities,
but it is the same God who works all in all"
and "...the Spirit is given to each one for the profit of all"

Sisters of Social Service—diverse enough in thought
to navigate and to negotiate,
to encompass and to embrace,
to heal and to hold,
to welcome the world!

If we listen, we establish, we empower, we set sail...

Sisters of Social Service, full speed ahead,
full and by, in Margaret's weatherly vessel![4]
Sisters of Social Service, her aggregate sail,
billow by God's grace, then, flank[5]
with the wind, the wind of the Spirit, moving upon the face of the waters!

Genesis 1:2, KJV
[2] Sr. Margaret Slachta, foundress of the Sisters of Social Service in Hungary
[3] lines 37-41, 1 Corinthians 12:4-7 NKJV
[4] nautical terms:
"full speed ahead" = moving as fast and quickly as possible;
"full and by" = sailing into the wind with care to keep the sails full, (figuratively) pursuing a
task with steady, unwavering engagement without unnecessary fuss or duress;
"weatherly" = easily maneuvered and sailed
[5] nautical term: "flank" = faster than "full speed"; maximum ship's speed

To My Delta Choraliers—Singing Sorors Singing Sisterhood
On the occasion of
the 50th Anniversary Concert
of the Los Angeles Delta Choraliers
May 24, 2008

(Dedicated to Soror Danellen Mabry Joseph, Founding Director,
whose very being Defines the Spirit and Tirelessness
of the Delta Choraliers)

What began in 1951 as the audacious desire of Undergrad Danellen Mabry
      to integrate the Greek Spring Fest at U.S.C.
      to champion the name of Delta Sigma Theta,

What began with a confluence of many daring collegiate sorors—
  singers and "lip-singers"
      to represent Upsilon Chapter
      to distinguish the name of Delta Sigma Theta,

What began with the dulcet tones of determined, "drum majorettes"—
      fourteen to fifteen young sonorous sorors singing sisterhood,

Blossomed into diapason slayers of Goliaths in 1952,
      a trophied "Honorable Mention" for Upsilon Chapter at 'S.C.'s
      "Spring Fest"
      participation for Pi Chapter at U.C.L.A.'s "Spring Sing"
      and the name of Delta Sigma Theta published on both campuses
      across the city

Blossomed into a seasonal subcommittee of Los Angeles Alumnae
  Chapter
      and, on the appointed day,
      Founders Day in 1958,
      a destined, christening day,
      appeared these singing sisters,
dubbed by Thelma Mitchell,
the "Delta Choraliers"—

Blossomed into a committed choir of singing sorors singing everywhere
        at National Conventions and Regional Conferences
        on long-playing, black vinyl records and cd's in two-album sets
        in settings for kinder and on campuses for collegiates
        and in centers for adults with very specialized needs
in churches and libraries,
in residences and halls,
in hospitals, hotels and big shopping malls

Blossomed into a legacy of commemorative concerts, honoring
Dr. Martin Luther King, Jr. for forty years
        connecting community to community
        sorority to sorority
        artistic torchbearers to youthful prodigy

The Delta Choraliers—our singing sorors singing sisterhood!

If you want to know what it means to be a Delta,
        spend time with these diamondiferous daystars—
        the Delta defilade—our singing sorors singing sisterhood

Among the Delta Choraliers is where I learned how to
        live life
        love life
        celebrate life
        share life
        respect life
        serve life
        sing life
        integrate life
        stay connected to life
        and even dream bigger life
        as a Delta

June 1982,
this baby Delta,
five months neophyte fresh across the sands,
at my first "Regional,"
encountered
the dateless, dapper, dancing, drumming, devoted, diplomatic,
disarming (and utterly charming) Danellen Mabry Joseph,

directing the Regional Chorus

First brief queries and comments back and forth:
      I remember,
           "Come to rehearsal."
           "Go home and get your black dress."
           "Can you be back by…"
What I did on the southbound Harbor Freeway mid-Friday afternoon
was only surpassed by what I did on the northbound Harbor Freeway
      returning to Pasadena
      in a Maverick with a V-8 engine
      driven by a twenty year old
      in love with curves.

Second queries and comments back and forth:
      I remember,
           "See Juanita Mc Namee, our librarian, about music."
           "We meet at Theresa Brown's house."
           "Come to rehearsal."
And, in September, I did…
once ahead of time, once on time (but soon learned better).

Thus, my lifelong formation began
as an undergrad among the grads…twice a month—
      an undergrad watching, gleaning, learning
      what dedicated life looked like
      through the eyes and acts of prophyte Deltas.

For some, everything they needed to know, they learned in kindergarten.*
For me, I kept on learning—learning from these singing sorors singing
  sisterhood

Among the Delta Choraliers is where I learned how to function in my
  Delta family
      with my sorors old and sorors new
      (my first and only
      hierarchically classic,
      yet classy and class-less society)
      with officers and ex-officers,
      up-and-comers and committee workers
      canvassed everywhere!

Among the Delta Choraliers is where I learned how to function in my
  extended Delta family
                 with the children of (now grand- and great-grand children
                    of, too),
                 siblings of, parents of, husbands of, more relatives of,
                 friends of, neighbors of, students of,
                 colleagues of, employers and employees of
                 my singing sorors singing sisterhood

Among the Delta Choraliers is where I learned how to be alive in Delta!
                 commitment and camaraderie,
                 capability and connectivity,
                 conscription and coercion
                 carpooling and commuting
                 cooperation and coordination
                 character and compassion
                 counsel and courage
                 comedy and...cookies—
    (Have mercy, I'd do anything for the promise of
    some of Miriam White's butter-baked sugar cookies...
    My mother can only guess how many were sent that she never
      saw... .)

If you want to know what it means to be a Delta,
              spend time with these diamondiferous daystars—
                 the Delta defilade

Among the Delta Choraliers is where I keep on learning—
        learning from my sisters ever singing sisterhood
so that fifty years from now,
I look forward to being alive again in Delta,
        reunited forever in $\Omega\Omega$ Chapter
          with so many beloveds "active" there.

Among my Delta Choraliers...
Among my sister Choraliers...
Among my singing sorors singing sisterhood!

* *All I Really Need to Know I Learned in Kindergarten* by Robert Fulghum

World View

"Clobberate" [1] —"That they may all be one…" [2]

(dedicated to all my Sisters and Sorors—S.S.S. and Delta Sigma Theta Sorority, Inc.)

STOP IT!
Seek Reconciliation

Acknowledge the hurt that happened
Deny it not
Diminish it not
Dismiss it not
Accept it
         and
Own it

Value and Validate your sister
Embrace each other with God's love

Release the hurt to God, true source of understanding, renewal, and
  liberation
for healing
for forgiveness
for the living
for the dead
for yourself

REPEAT   REPEAT   REPEAT
as much as necessary
    with whomever necessary [3]
        until reconciled
            because it is necessary
                that you may have life and live life more abundantly. [4]

---

[1] combination of "cooperate" and "clobber"; word coined by Jane Levikow, formerly a Sister of Social Service
[2] John 17:21 (NRSV-CE New Revised Standard Version, Catholic Edition)
[3] Begin with God; then the individual(s) involved one-by-one, with or without a supportive mediator/mediating team; if the individual is unavailable, then with a supportive mediator/mediating team; end with God. If approached for reconciliation as a participant or mediator, remember, "Blessed are the peacemakers, for they shall be called the sons (and daughters) of God." Matt. 5:9
[4] John 10:10 (NKJB–New King James Bible)

Contemplating Caritas
John 14: 15-20

My Lord's
inside me
inside Him
inside the Father
inside me
inside Him
inside me
inside the Temple of the Holy Spirit
inside me
inside Three
inside me
inside God
My Lord!

Grey* in a Black and White World

My world has always been black and white
(no gray areas)

First BLACK
Then BLACK with a white outline
Then WHITE with a black center
Then BLACK with white on top and
WHITE with black on the bottom
Then WHITE with intermittent black spots,
which were, in reality, polka dots
(that someone conveniently had whited out)

In response, my world turned solid BLACK

Then BLACK with an ominous white shadow
Then WHITE with a black stripe
IN   THE   MIDDLE
Then BLACK with a white strip in between
Then BLACK with intermittent white spots,
which were roughly splattered polka dots
(that I inserted AND DISCOVERED MADE A MESS)

In response, I tried to blend the colors (of my world)
The more I mixed, the more they divided

First BLACK with white in an upper corner
Then WHITE with black in a lower corner
Then WHITE with an ominous black shadow

I even tried to add
some RED once
with a pint of BROWN
and a touch of YELLOW

THEY   WERE   ABSORBED

—lost somewhere
—embedded in the blackness (probably)

The more my world changed, the more it stayed the same

MY WORLD HAS ALWAYS BEEN BLACK AND WHITE

(no gray areas)

but
sometimes,
on a day like today,
I feel
completely
grey.

* variation of "gray," defined as intermediate in condition, etc.

Looking Down on the Moon

The moon...
cold, remote, mercurial
a secondary yet relentless gravitational force,
constant in its inconsistency,
does what it does
in its own time
in its own way
with its own unfathomable purpose
as indifferent to me as I am to it,
if I happen to catch a glimpse of it
while driving home at night,
and, every glimpse, too, is variable
from turn to turn on the road

Easy to dismiss thinking about the moon
More important "variables"
preoccupy me behind the wheel
I'm already distracted
by 'mid-March madness of the worst kind

The natural strikes me as unnatural, off, unnaturally off—
with the younger sister of my mother,
the one full of rough life and raucous laughter,
the one whose name Mother calls me when I laugh with abandon,
the one Mother silenced from public emoting by calling her name
  at Grandmother's funeral,
the one who redeemed an abusive marriage
with boiling water and a glowing 18" cast iron frying pan,
who raised a veterinarian-to-be gone assistant,
a business woman nearly a preacher
and a cop musician, fathering next generation musicians of family legacy,
        passed away
She is the first of her generation making the transition,
the first of Mother's actual sisters and brother,
to join our ancestors
I make it there "a day late..." after she
        passed
We've prayed for many who've been "low"; they've recovered

Didn't even know she was *that* sick the day I left.

Their generation tells my generation nothing
We still have to "overhear grown folks" talking,
though there ain't but four
of them "grown" womenfolk left now—
one top of the hill, one bottom of the hill,
one running the cafe at the corner just 'round the way
and one clear across the country three thousand miles
The closer they are, the less they seem to speak
civilly to one another
although everyone talks to Mother—the "Mediator"
(some more than others),
the one clear across the country three thousand miles,
usually pre-dawn on West Coast, L.A. time,
maybe because they know
she's safer than Fort Knox,
holds things in her heart like Jesus' mother,
maintains the neutrality of Switzerland,
negotiates more diplomatically than Henry Kissinger
and speaks truth graciously enough to make anyone say,
"That was so beautiful! Curse me out again."

Don't know whether it's harder on her or me,
watching this strong, brilliant, soft-spoken,
well-educated Black woman
succumb to the ravages of a lifetime,
working too hard too long
before reaching puberty until years after retirement
combined with a truck, then van car accidents

What must Mother, silent, looking out
her kitchen window, feel, looking at
but not seeing the "Worm Moon"?*
It must be harder on her.
How it aches me, too
I stay the course,
do what I do,
with purpose, controlled,
for her sake

...and mine

My mother is in her seventies, delicate, feisty,
wanting but unable to travel the three thousand miles
to perform "last rites" as the eldest sister,
so I go,
(her one and only)
home to the homestead
home to North Carolina
home to Lenoir
home to Freedman
home to the family's Methodist church
home to the "new cemetery"
somewhatly masked as integrated

Seems we've only made it back
for funerals my whole adult life,
if I don't count freshman year
at her Alma Mater, Bennett College,
but who's really considered an adult at eighteen
by family, outside of parental threatening
or recounting all the milestones made,
rites of passage checked off,
obstacles overcome
or dreams rearranged
by the time an elder "was your age."

I'm commissioned
to remember my training,
my mission to "be a lady,"
the "dignified daughter of the 'Ambassador' "

I stay with the eldest elder,
in the home of my early childhood,
reminiscing about my one-two-three-four-year old's adventures
and reconnecting with my older cousins
I remember as "big kids"
or baby sitters already in high school
I play my role—the "substitute" mediator—,
trying to get cousins from my generation

friendly walking and talking,
sitting and sipping together
over restaurant meals
if for no other reason than
it's "Aunt Bett's daughter" visiting,
innocent and young
(even at forty something)
believing, "She doesn't know"
about the real family feuds
'twixt our mothers and grandmothers,
'tween sister and sister
and sister and niece
and nephew and Great-Uncle,
          passed on
cousin to cousin to cousin
and so on,
beyond when the original parties
          passed on.
It ain't no game.
It's serious.
It's vicious.
It's potentially violent.
Nobody fights like family
All survivors bear deep, ugly scars
          passed on.
This ambassador must be
careful where she stays
careful what she says
careful with what she hears
careful with what she shares
Be positive,
be supportive,
be silent
or be gone.

I volunteer; they decide to let me
proof and edit the funeral program
with my Aunt's daughter,
whose maybe nine years my senior.
Hungry wolves sniff to see

if I am a part of their pack
or should they tear me apart?
Always ready to try anyone,
teeth bared at somebody
I disarm solely by wit, humor and tactful discretion
not to mention
hilarious-to-them mistakes
(because I really don't know
a lot of family intrigue nor intricacies)
        and
endearing-to-an-individual connections
because I repeat and repeat,
in hopes of dressing a festering wound,
"We're kin. We're blood. We're family."

Success! A few cousins swap
dead for currently active phone numbers
and laugh, recounting notoriously elaborate
picture stealing escapades
among our elders, living and deceased

Consolation and resurrection
exchange places
with anger, resentment, hurt
in common grieving
over the precious loss of life...
at least temporarily
until the next raw "incident"

This unnetted tightrope of neutrality,
more than any time changes,
is exhausting

I fly home in one piece—
whole with a hole in my heart—
feeling the relentless gravitational pull
of no time for this bereaved to grieve,
cold, devoid of life, yet mercurial
in my private inconsistency

My "debrief" with Mother
does what it does
in its own time
in its own way
with its own purpose
as I hand her a still cold
from the suitcase
copy of the program,
and leave her to "the Obituary (Read Silently),"
while I collapse into surface sleep
worthless to the undead
because I must prepare for work the next day.

Then, more 'mid-March madness of the worst kind
strikes when the phone rings
much too early
in a much too short conversation
Mother with my cousin, I soon find out
The matriarch of the family
            passed,
the last of her generation,
the one Mother grew up with as the "baby sister"
in her grandmother's house,
the grandmother she thought was her mother,
my youngest Great-Aunt
I am closest to her children:
older ones babysat me,
read to me, got me to walk;
the boys hung around my dad,
talking cars, sports and other male things
I even planned to marry one
of them when I was two
(Jealous moments passed
when I attended his wedding);
some came to visit us in L.A.,
alone or with family.

We almost always stayed or visited with them
whenever we returned South;
the two youngest, closest to me in age,

I played with, confided in,
and was even allowed, on occasion,
a few minutes to speak, quasi-privately,
on the phone with,
during those expensive, extensive
you got charged every partial minute
for distance and time by Ma Bell
landline calls on the house's hallway phone.
(They all knew the "family ring code"
to be sure someone picked up
if we were home during "normal" hours.)
I guess, in actuality, they are Mother's
  first cousins and my seconds
and their kids, my thirds with fourths and fifths,
but I learned them as firsts
and related to their mother as Mother's sister

So, I go back
to the homestead,
to the "passed on" eldest elder's house
with repacked funeral clothes
I had to buy after landing last trip
I go back
to represent Mother,
now this tribe's Matriarch
I go back
a bit better prepared,
but not really,
and stay with my cousin, now become my sister
I sing in tribute at this service,
and find out the church musician, of course,
is another cousin on some side through somebody
I hear my grandmother's touch in her fingertips...

From a funeral program,
I discover there is a "claimed" half-brother
and figure right then and there
it will take a lifetime for me to sort it out,
let alone attach all the names in my head
to the faces before me, in my mind or in re-possessed pictures,

and I don't even care because I,
who have grown up so very far away from all of them,
really believe, really hope, really trust in:
"We're kin. We're blood. We're family."

Exhausted far greater than the sick leave days
combined with my "Personal Emergency Leave" days tally,
I take the red-eye and fly home—
whole with fractured pieces and a bigger hole in my heart —

cold, distant, devoid of life, devoid of time
still with the purpose
to do what I do:
to get back to my mother
to go back to life's home away from home
to get back to my classroom
to reassure my "kids" they're ready
for state-wide testing starting shortly after dawn
to pray Spring Break gets here sooner
in abbreviated calendar days
to get back
      to my mother
          to myself

I stare out the window
—all I can manage—
tired beyond sleep, weary, devoid,
eyes fixate on the dark echoing my dark,
searching for stars to fire hope,
disperse fear, ignite understanding,
still the rising flood of "Why?"

Drawn to pay attention to what I notice least,
drawn by a secondary yet relentless gravitational pull,
remote, cold, emotionally indifferent,
I lean forward
and glance down on the moon,
not shifting, not changing, not moving around,
different from earthbound views when I have looked
through car windows or over urban rooftops

or through neighborhood backyard trees
Looking down on the moon,
the unnatural strikes me as natural, yet off,
unnaturally big, naturally beautiful, naturally off somehow,
imperceptible and slow,
determined to defy
right reason, right vision, right mind
Leaning forward, for a better view
through that oval quadruple pane,
eyes lock, brain locks on an orb,
seemingly locked in synch
with this fellow object moving across its sky
Looking down on the moon
I do what I do,
rely on logic
to give respite to one lost
in the topsy-turvy
broken looking glass reflection
of life without...
without enough time
to get to say, "Get well,"
let alone to say, "Goodbye"
Desperate for distraction,
I keep looking down on the moon
until its power pulls me unconscious

Ten days, two trips, two aunts, two generations,
two burials, two plane tickets solo

What must poor Mother, silent, looking out
her kitchen window, feel,
looking at but not seeing...
It must be harder on her.
How it aches me, too

> *God, what were You thinking?*
> *What are You doing?*
> *Do You feel what we feel?*

Days later, back at my church in the big city,

after an 8 a.m. homily on "Lazarus"**
forces me to take a moment
of distracted Lenten reflection,
outer silence before the Tabernacle
stills repetition of my internal screaming:

> *God, what are You thinking?*
> *What are You doing?*
> *Do You feel how we feel...really?*

In the instant I close my eyes,
I see that moon—full, refulgent,
that moon still with me, still strikes me
that moon, with its natural beauty so unnaturally off,
and my inner ear hears Haydn's strains
of "The Heavens Are Telling the Glory of God"
It dawns on and unearths me, disinters me:
> We don't look *down* on the moon
> It doesn't stand constant in the sky
> It doesn't companion us, follow us on our journeys

I remember, I exhale, I sit still...
in the silence and listen
to the high pitched ringing in my inner ear.

I hear from our Creator:
> "The Man in Jesus wept for His friend;
> the God in Jesus raised him!"

Then, the disconsolate soul of the distraught
within me, uses that moment's tears
to release *something*,
to console *something*,
to renew *something*,
and I am comforted:

I know Your thoughts are not my thoughts
I know Your ways are not my ways. ***
I know You know what You are doing.
Yes, You do feel what we feel.

Yes, You care
...even if Your thoughts are not my thoughts,
even if Your ways are not my ways... .

Divine mantra replaces the broken record of so many days' rant,
yielding calm, yielding solace, yielding peace...

but it's still hard for those of us left here,
left to carry on here—
some days more than others
some moments more than others
some years more than others
some seasons more than others
some months more...
some moments more...

Yet, the Maker of the universe,
Creator of heaven and earth,
deigned to reach out,
looking down on me,
struck natural, unnatural and unnaturally off,
and set in motion—
using the relentless, gravitational force
of God's own constancy
in God's own time
in God's own way
with God's own power and purpose—
the genesis of healing
in the wee, darkest hours of morning
as I stared through an airplane window,
and leaned forward,
looking down on the moon

*Full moon in March
**John 11:1-45
***Isaiah 55: 8-9

My Answer Is "Yes"

Lord, if You are asking,
" 'Can you give your life to Me,' " *
   then my answer is "yes"—
        "yes" with no "but's,"
        "yes" because I trust You…
            and Your love for me
                beyond my fears and limitations.

My answer is "yes"
—the "yes" of the doubter, the skeptic, the pragmatist
        I am the "yes" of Thomas

My answer is "yes"
—the "yes" of the impatient, the stubborn, the brash
        I am the "yes" of Peter

My answer is "yes"
—the "yes" of the bold, the temperamental, the wild, the angry
        I am the thundering sons of Zebedee,
            storming more inside than out
            wielding empowerment given by You
            seeking leadership governed by You

My answer is "yes"
—the "yes" of the child, the idealist, the innocent,
  the vulnerable, the anxious, the misinterpreted,
 the passionate, the loving
        I am the "yes" of John,
            another "beloved" sheep among the wolves,
                desiring most to be with You
                striving more and more to emulate You
                needing always the security of Your arms
                learning again and again the assurance of Your
                  voice
                seeking only the peace of laying my head on Your
                  bosom

and putting my heart in Your hands

I am a swirling, whirling, frothy blend of them all
and a little bit more (...known only by You)!

I am Your kid sister**, Betty**
I love You, too...
     and my answer is "yes!"

*from "The Kingdom Is Free," music and lyrics by Sister Rebecca Shinas, O.P.
** Permission to insert your gender appropriate term and your name or nickname is
granted by the poet <u>for personal affirmation use only.</u>

On Twenty-One

Seven days of Twenty-one
For once, I feel the difference:

No longer a child, nor even a teen
Stepped over the brink of disaster

Fought the hard fight against growing up
while dabbling with adulthood.
        —played the child who was mature
        —played the teen who could endure

Strong convictions wrote the scripts
        approved by God.
I liked the roles and made them one,
a part I knew so well.
After all, they'd been a "smashing hit"
two decades and a year.

Director's been hinting, last few seasons,
the roles would soon play out

Said He had a new angle of emphasis:
        "Let the woman show!"
        "Let adulthood out!"

"No," I cried.
"I want no part in this!
I'm a Peter Pan player 'til I die.
There is no success like success... ."

Bonds redeemed, assurances guaranteed,
the curtain closed its last,
and, in my dressing room
on the bureau,
I found
a brand-new script.

PRAYER REQUEST
Part I

Just pray—

Pray for those who ask
Pray for those who can not
Pray for those who know that they need it
Pray for those who do not
Pray for those who want help
Pray for those who do not
Pray for those who believe
Pray for those who do not

Pray for us all—
        in the past
        in the present
        in the future

Amen.

PRAYER REQUEST
Part II

Just pray—

Pray for those who can ask for it
Pray for those who will ask not... more
Pray for those who desire help
Pray for those who specifically desire it not...more
Pray for those who know they need it
Pray for those who especially know not their need of it...more
Pray for those who fervently believe in its power
Pray for those who firmly believe it to no avail more

Pray for all—
       in the past
       in the present
       in the future...more

Amen.

The Senses
(Gifts to Relish Life)

One mouth…
One nose…
Eyes and ears –
a pair of those –
But twice five fingers
and ten toes…

Ponder well God's gifts!

"The Senses," Poet's Commentary

Talk the least!
Smell just a bit more
lest we get too lost in anything
Breath and breathing,
constant flowing in and out
of God and self;
hence, two nostrils
Look and listen
twice as much
Touch, Feel, Do
ten times as much.

Talk

I need to talk to someone,
but who that someone is…?
      I…DON'T…KNOW

I cannot talk to you—
You are human
I can not *talk* to you!
Humans do not understand,
and often confuse the issue.

I need to talk to someone,
but who that someone is…?
      I…DON'T…KNOW

I cannot talk to my dog—
It listens
I can not *talk* to my dog.
It does not understand and
is hurt because it cannot respond
to my pain

I need to talk to someone,
but who that someone is…?
      I…DON'T…KNOW

I cannot talk to me—
I am only human
I can not *talk* to me!
I listen. I understand.
I respond with empathetic frustration,
but I have not the vision of solution!

I need to talk to someone,
but who that someone is…?
I really know…
He is the same One
that I've talked to in troubled times before
He listens. He understands.
He is the Power of Solution.

I only need to speak.

Why do I AVOID Him—
        not rid myself of pain?!!

I need to talk to someone
and Who that someone is…
        I know.

Warrior

I am a warrior
born of warrior stock
from many tribes
and many lands,
   known and unknown

I know some about warrior Grandpapa Charlie
   my Cherokee paternal great-grandfather,
   who hid out in the mountains
of West Virginia and North Carolina with others
not all part of "the people,"
"human beings," trying to escape the "Trail of Tears"
   I recently learned he killed a white man in a fight
   No other warrior details, except he liked nobody
   and foretold his own death to the season

My maternal great-grandfather, Henry T., was a warrior
   son of the enslaved,
   volunteered for the Spanish American War,
then, fought to eke out a living
as a traveling African American musician
on weekends in the South

My father was a warrior
in the not labeled a war, "Korean Conflict"
but had to fight even harder
alongside my warrior mother
when he returned
to get Disabled American Veteran benefits,
across three states, across this country,
finally decreed "96%,"
anything and everything to reduce potentialities,
but his warrior family survived and thrived,
was housed and educated,
even after he died at age 47,
in a V.A. hospital,
from service-connected fallout,
leaving a widow and child
away from all family.

The blood in my veins—
       hot and icy
The paint on my face—
       visible and invisible
The genetics I pass on—
       verbal and microbial
             are those of a warrior

It's who I am
It's what I do
       for God and God's family
       for justice more than "just us"
       for fallen warriors,
             who fought before me
       for rising warriors,
             who train to take my place
       for all my tribes,
             known and unknown.

I
AM
A
WARRIOR!

Wash of Ocean Sentiment

The waves of time are lapping at my shore,
a slow progression smoothing off a picture
drawn roughly—memories etched in my sand.

Serrated edges change their snags for round
Lines crooked in life's warp and woof skew straight
Surf's crest, relentless, gently buffs each spike
while draining harshness in the foam of tide.

The waves of time are lapping at my shore,
abrasion quickly changing a life's moment
pressed deeply as a mem'ry in my sand.

Impressions good and bad in rock pools churn
Fogged morning dims true sight within mind's eye
Wraith portraits shine a fractured light of truth,
false life bestowed by ocean sentiment.

Social Commentary

Are You Grieving in Heaven?

Are you grieving in heaven,
Mothers, Grandmothers and Great-Grandmothers?
Are you grieving in heaven?++
> *In Ramah was there a voice heard,*
> *lamentation and weeping and great mourning,*
> *Rachel weeping for her children*
> *and would not be comforted,*
> *because they are no more.*[1]

This week in Texas, at Robb School (2022), nineteen elementary babies
> slain by a teenage baby
> slain by police,
> who stood idly by during the assault

Then, there was Coleman High School (1970) in Arkansas and
49th Street Elementary School (1984) in California and
Oakland Elementary School (1988) in South Carolina and
Cleveland Elementary School (1989) in California and
Lindhurst High School (1992) in California and
Frontier Middle School (1996) in Washington and
Pearl High School (1997) in Mississippi and
Heath High School (1997) in Kentucky and
Thurston High School (1998) in Oregon and
Westside Middle School (1998) in Arkansas and
Colombine High School (1999) in Colorado and
Santana High School in California (2001) and
Red Lake Senior High School in Minnesota (2005) and
West Nickel Mines School in Pennsylvania (2006) and
Sandy Hook Elementary School in Connecticut (2012) and
Marshall County High School (2018) in Kentucky and
Marjory Stoneman Douglass High School (2018) in Florida and
Santa Fe High School (2018) in Texas and
Oxford High School (2021) in Michigan and
the plethora of all those untrumpeted shots in and around
"economically disadvantaged and 'at risk' '' schools
  (code for *schools comprised dominantly of poor children of color*)

and all those babies slain

Are you grieving in heaven?
Is that why all the clouds gather
                heavy and gray?
Is that the source of torrential flooding, flash flooding, heart flooding
—a deluge of tears conceived in the cosmos

Then, there is the onslaught of war—
                tribal, national, racial, political, medical,
                        germicidal, genocidal, agricultural, aqua-centric, ...
                GLOBAL—
                slaying our children
                in Africa and Haiti and Ukraine and Palestine and Israel and
                Afghanistan and so many other "stans,"
                and, especially, in the Americas,
                the United States of America
                        racists slaying my people
                        police slaying my people
                        politicos and power-mongers slaying the people
                        platoons of paid predators and
                        purveyors of lies slaying the people
the hurt hurting the hurt (and vulnerable)...burgeoning
children slaying other children and themselves
and their elders and their people
parents slaying children slaying parents,
                scattering potentialities to the wind

And how we assault all life, all elements, all creation—
                the animals, the land, the waters, the atmosphere!
We clamor over machinations for moon, stars and planets,
                whatever we can reach
                in our mind's and technological eye.
Are we as relentless as we are repentless?

Are You grieving, Most Holy of Holy,
>in heaven, in earth, in us, in all creation?
Do we commit the unforgivable sin, blaspheming Your gifts
>with our actions, speaking wordless volumes,
>grieving You, Holy Spirit, Eternal Mother of All Existence?
Remember Your mercy
Regather us
Reinvigorate Your love
>within and among us
>so that we, Your children in the chrysalis[2],
>mirror You in renewing our face of the cosmos—
>the earth

[1]Matthew 2:18, 21st Century King James Bible
[2]Elbert Hubbard, "We Are Gods in the Chrysalis."

Autochthonous*

I trust you not. I cast your constant lies aside
because you think you have all privilege and pride
from what you see your world, so small, spew back to you.
But, I've got news. Take off the blinders, rosy hued.
The peoples of the world connect the continents
as one primordial memory itself re-knits
the fabric of the masses nearby and remote;
demanding voices rise for place, boots off their throat!
The day approaches faster than tsunamic floods
to rend, rebuild, restore new bounties from first bloods.

*of or from an inhabitant of a place; indigenous rather than descended from
migrants or colonists

Campin' or Trampin'

Whoever said getting back to nature is good for you
wasn't from my "neck of the 'hood."
Have you ever been campin'?
        sleepin' out under the stars
        on the ground
        in a sleeping bag
        worrying 'bout some creepy crawlies
        in between yo' blankets
        mosquitos biting
        chiggers itching
        no hot water
        no plumbin' for yo' plumbin'
        not even a "Port-o-Potty" to piss in
        maybe a tent
        and some dried, tasteless re-hydratable rations
        older than stuff my dad called,
        "hard tack" from the Korean Conflict
My Great-Grandmomma in the South
        at least had a "crick" for water behind her shack,
        so she and the rest of the family
        didn't have to hike a country mile for "sweet water"
her place, much bigger than these cottages for counselors
and definitely much better than these open-to-the-air tin roofed,
look like a lean-to to me contraptions,
        complete with splintering wood outhouse
        and one "orange water" water fountain
        for "regular" guests, youth groups and company schmoes
her place, not as big as the two split-level lodges reserved for…

Who'd you say gets those? For how much?
Oh, VIP accommodations—for Boss and executive staff

No…   thank…   you…

I know life in the city,
in downtowns
and gentrifying 'round towns

where the homeless "live"
for free but not so *free,*
plagued by four-legged coyotes
and roaming two legged dogs
and snakes, stealing blankets
not to keep warm but to follow the scent
of cold white dust,
laced cigarettes
or something else…,
where gleaning water,
cleanest from rain,
more often comes from a building's unlocked spigot
with or without a hose someone left out.

Have fun "Trampin'"

No…   thank…   you…

I ain't goin' "Campin'" ever again
…and, no, I ain't plannin' no family vacation
at the company paid "Animal Farm" co-op
or dude ranch, either.

ESCAPE from SLAVERY

They are slaves.
They are Black.
Like vines creeping
through the undergrowth,
they silently steal away
from the plantations
through the night

Then, the noise,
the awful, sickening
howls of hounds
close in pursuit
These slaves go
on and on,
running for their lives,
these hard-pressed antelope
long removed from Africa.

They reach the swamps,
wading desperately,
holding on
to their babies.
Suddenly, there are
the masters,
the overseers,
the bloodhounds.

BANG!
Guns blast!
Screams of the dying
go underwater.
The whites kill some,
but they can't
hold nor haul
them all
back.
They must be
FREE!

Left to Languish

With Father, Son and Spirit, life we ford
dependent on Your way and promise, Lord
Through rapids, rivers, oceans, swamps, we've poured
O'er mountains, deserts, valleys, storms we've soared

Triangulating You, evil we bored,
and following Your light, advanced and scored
each victory miraculously won
For who can stand against God's firstborn Son,
Who won the war on Cal'vry's darkest day,
so skirmishes we fight, ne'er hold full sway
o'er any person bowed in prayer and praise,
relying on Your help, folds hands, arms raise

Devalued, disrespected by World's horde,
misused, abused, betrayed, hollowed and cored,
ne'er left to languish is Your promise, Lord

'Tis comfort knowing every place we're gored,
each slash, each tear, each piercing by a sword,
You mark and dress and bind and heal each ward
for that is what You promise us, sweet Lord

Weak, battle weary, wounded, left, ignored,
we trust Your promise not to languish, Lord
From trampled spirits, dreams almighty soared
For any person bowed in praise and prayer,
can cast aside hell's fire, release all care

You ferry us triumphant 'til we're shored,
redeemed, and resurrected! Yes, restored!

Both Lion and lioness of Judah roared
from Jericho's downed walls; God's children board
Your freedom train, fares paid! Fete, "Drinking Gourd!"
Left not to languish is Your promise, Lord

In counting costs paid here, we would not hoard
to risk to see Your face, O, radiant Lord
You warned the world would deem us, "albatross"
We, witnesses, be nailed upon a cross
by lies and schemes its lackeys ever toss,
possessed by world's fake gleam and fading gloss
Ne'er left to languish, orphaned nor ignored
for that is not Your way nor promise, Lord

Each sacrifice here moves me with another—
a sister, child, an elder or a brother—
to seek the peace and joy that You award
through truth and love—Your way—, so thank You, Lord

O, bless companions, sojourners by grace,
who raise us out of pitfalls in this race
to help cross hurdles steady in a pace,
so we, like Paul, begin along the way
to say, "We've done a lap, kept faith today."
Ne'er left to languish, orphaned nor ignored,
we trust Your promise not to languish, Lord

We praise Your Name in song; with every chord
and word, ring out Your glories, precious Lord,
until in full communion we move toward
eternal praise and worship, our reward!
Infinity of reasons You're adored
and why we offer all we can afford—
our life and living, love in service, Lord,
and, with forgiving, preach with one accord
we trust Your promise not to languish, Lord

All praise to Father, Spirit, Son adored!
All praise to Blessed Trinity adored!
We know and stand on truth! Your way brings life,
rejuvenation in the midst of strife
Ne'er left to languish, orphaned nor ignored,
with Father, Son and Spirit, life we ford

Nope. Never Been to Camp

Watching my parents and most everybody else's parents
bust their buns to keep any roof over our heads,
then proudly moving up from apartments
to triplexes to duplexes to single family two bedrooms/one bath houses,
small for a "nuclear" three, and
smaller if more kin with kids showed up
(I think they call them "starters homes" now)
My parents started to convert a closet to a half bath
when I hit high school, but then Dad passed and
Mom joined him long after her retirement.
Decades later, I am starting up
the same conversion conversation,
but looking warily at contractors
and leerily at bankrupted company pension funds,
figuring…and figuring
how to keep my parents' roof,
(just replaced the tile for the first time)
over my head,
praying and hoping I won't fall prey,
these cascading years,
to developers
and gentrifiers
and "eminent domainers,"
displacing so many seniors,
widows and widowers,
lost job-ers and too-many-job-ers,
who look like me,
like the family, moving the car
block to block each night,
or like the RV-er, moving
from the beach
to the church curb
to the cemetery wall.
Ain't no backpack big enough
for a human to carry
all this inside load outside.
We've passed bonds—

"BB" and "CC" and "GG"
and the city and county and state
still get a "Fail, UU"
on their report cards
for what we haven't seen funds doing.
The homeless continue
in "encampments" tented in the great outdoors—
      parks, benches, beaches, sidewalks,
      steps, open lots and bushes;
others seek quasi-indoor accommodations—
      underpasses, stairwells, "For Sale" homes,
      abandoned and partially renovated buildings.

It's no wonder my parents never sent me
to "Summer Camp," "Church Camp," or
any other overnighters…

and that was then,
when homelessness
used to be rare.

One's Own Culture, Part I

Know it
Respect it
Enjoy it
Extend it
Exceed it

Do anything
but
Forget it

One's Own Culture, Part II

See it
Squeeze it
Hear it
Breathe it
Smell it
Taste it
Feel it
Learn it
Live it
Love it
Circumnavigate it
Escape it
Elevate it

One's Own Culture,
Part III

Woo it!
Espouse it
Marry it!
Promote it
Protect it
Evoke it
Discuss it

Sing it
Swing it
Dance it
Chant it
Paint it
Carve it
Sculpt it
Perform it
Portray it

Be it
Pass it
Preserve it

Use it or lose it

One's Own Culture,
Part IV

Expand it
Exceed it
Just remember
its inextricable
sometimes,
inexplicable,
sometimes,
irrepressible,
sometimes,
irascible,
always
inherently,
inherited part
won't part
from you.

W.D.J.D.—<u>W</u>hat <u>D</u>id <u>J</u>esus <u>D</u>o? [1]

Would He rip babies from Mothers' and Fathers' arms
deporting the mature, often to face hired death squads
caging young ones without records
nullifying the possibility of re-unification
this side of heaven,
killing hopes, killing dreams—
a modern day Ramah[2] ?

What does Jesus do? He cries with me; He cries over you.
Is it Christian? Is it something He taught us to do?

Would He lie in wait at elementary school graduations
or college libraries or nearby coffee houses
or places of employment or courtroom hallways
or violate the sanctity of houses of prayer
to snatch persons with
        differing skin tones
        differing speech
        differing dress
        differing ethnicities
        differing histories
        differing holidays and holy days
        differing life and living styles
and   differing traditions?

What does Jesus do? He cries with me; He cries over you.
Is it Christian? Is it something He taught us to do?

Would He slam to the ground or choke, taze or shoot the life's breath
  from anyone, the very Ruah from His own Spirit freely given?

Would He dismiss, defile, degrade, defame
anyone without opening the door
to reconciliation, restoration and rehabilitation?

Would He proffer peace kissing righteousness
or would He consort with war-mongers,

who plunder peoples and planet for profit and might?

What does Jesus do? He cries with me; He cries over you.
Is it Christian? Is it something He taught us to do?

Did He recite His people's whole history and reveal hidden mysteries,
or did He re-write, reduce and encrypt the truth?
Did He come for one or come for all?
Did He say, "Embrace only yourself, your friends and your family"
or did He re-define societal notions
of neighbor, class, gender, status and leadership?

What does Jesus do? He cries with me; He cries over you.
Is it Christian? Is it something He taught us to do?

Did He relish all creation held in His Hands
from the mustard seed to the Sea of Galilee,
elevating humans with His Incarnation as one of us,
converting the breaking of bread
and the drinking of wine
into His sacred sacrificial Self?

What does Jesus do? He cries with me; He cries over you.
Is it Christian? Is it something He taught us to do?

Did He model God's intent for being
authentically human?
Would mercy and truth meet to season justice[3]
or would He preach the Philosophy of "Just us"?

What would Jesus do?
Certainly isn't what we see people do!

He reduced the Ten Commandments
down to two
for those who call themselves His followers:

> "Love God with all your heart, soul, mind and strength
> and love your neighbor as yourself." [4]

Call yourself a Christian? Is this what you do?
Does what Jesus did
describe you?

1 "W.D.J.D.—What Did Jesus Do" is a variation of the popular expression, "W.W.J.D.—What
Would Jesus Do"

2 Jeremiah 31:15

3 William Shakespeare, *Merchant of Venice* (IV, i)

4 Luke 10:27

When All You Can Do Isn't Enough

When you've lost your first job
because Covid opened up and the business closed up,
and your third side hustles, Uber and Lyft,
no longer work
because you can't afford California gas
and what little you buy
has to get you to job two, now your only…
and last through the long line of cars
for free bags of fruit and vegetables on Wednesday morning
and, possibly, a free box of meat, cereal and canned goods on Saturday

When your eldest is lying,
saying she's not that hungry,
and, "Give it to Junior,"
and school closes this week,
so no breakfasts and lunches
and you already know you won't make the rent in two weeks
with the eviction bans lifted
and rent assistance ended
Section 8? You're on the list.
It's not come through.
        You have done all you can do,
        and it isn't enough…
You consider, for the longest moment,
going back
just for a few weeks
He has a job…and a place
You can endure anything,
put up with anything
'til you get your bearings
and another "second job"
maybe online so you can watch the kids this summer
while he's at work
Oh, sh—t! Kid graduated 4th and turned in the Chromebook.
Maybe there'll be summer school this year
at the new intermediate…and maybe a new laptop.
That would leave you with only junior at home.

Then, you remember
you thought you caught him eyeing
baby girl not like a daughter,
lingering far, too long
at the bathroom door—spying
when you got home bandaged from the free clinic.
No, no never back there,
and you think,
"How long can we make it in the car?"
        when all you can do
        to try and make it through
        isn't enough.

***

I've done everything I'm supposed to do—
love my wife,
support my family
got a career now
got us out of that slum lord's apartment
rented a house,
helped make it a home
for my kids, for my family
started saving up for my girl's "Quince" in a few years
taught my boy fútbol and football
and both of them how to catch
and ride bikes,
but my manhood's in question
by me, their dad
Their papá could not protect them
from a fool with a gun,
who shot up their school
My babies won't be playing catch tonight
My wife's upstairs, watching, praying and crying
in the children's wing with mi'ja
in a "medically induced coma"
I'm standing here in the morgue, identifying
what's left of mi'jo
barely nine, barely recognizable,

looking like a bloodless, gutted victim of war
How can I be there
for my daughter, for my wife, for myself
Inside and out, this homey is dying.
        When all you can do
        to try and make it through
        isn't enough…

                                    ***

What time is it? What day is it? What year is it?
Covid has done a number on us all
Sense of season—unnatural
here existing "above ground and vertical"
Sense of time—imperceptible
blur-rage, passing
trying to maintain staying sane
amidst all the inane
and the dangerous
and the evil
and the in denial of plain truth
Wondering any moment of any given day
how you managed to do any fraction
of what you do now,
trying to care-take 24/7 and
teach five classes a day online
with weekly meetings and daily school reports
and constant calls to schedule
at-home visits for mother
and argue with an idiot doctor
who cannot see why you
will not bring a 92-year old,
barely mobile, to the hospital
for an appointment
in the height of a pandemic

She's elderly and she's Black
and to you and your system—
expendable—written off

as a liability better off dead
To me, she is my queen, daughter of the High King,
My mother, matriarch of one and endless generations,
so I call medical supervisors
and "Membership Services"
and learn from my students (also hers until bedridden)
how to upload photos from my camera phone
to a computer many years older than they are
and I fuss and I fight
simply trying to get people to do what's right
—show up when scheduled
—bring all needed supplies
watching things in a downward acceleration
calling and calling to get authorizations from her Primary Care
  Physician
(which worked out best on his vacations)
Home Health *can* provide
a wound specialist's visits
and dual nurses
and help secure
palliative care and hospice care—
gleaning truths
about what is what
and what is available
and *what should have been* offered
from sources other than
those who should provide
the information in the first place
until my queen lies gasping out her last breaths,
overmedicated until she
walks no more
eats no more
drinks no more
speaks no more
and, finally, breathes no more,
and I discover
all the nurses' weekly Home Health Care photos
never were shared with her physician
(his sub let it slip),

only the occasional photos I sent
with a "what's-the-delay" question were
in my queen's chart
Guilty! GUILTY! All guilty!

On his returning from vacation
the doctor wanted to make up
a reason for her death
to complete the certificate
(No blood pressure issues for more than three weeks!
I should know. I was there.
See my records, paramedics' records, home health nurses' records... .)
Guilty! GUILTY! All guilty
while I'm left empty
Our house, my house—left empty
except for the pain
and the rage
and the grief

and all the pain
because in your emptied heart of hearts
burning trenches in your mind
        you know you did all you could do
        (and as her "only" all you had was you)
        to try and make it through
        and it wasn't enough

Ignorance *ain't* bliss! Who told that lie?
Ignorance is expensive. Knowledge has power.
And lawyers have knowledge.
Let them wield it for *you* and all who look like *you*,
so no one else
spends another day
feels the anguish
because the HMO's gotten away
with it, yet again
Let lawyers do what they can do
and, maybe when they get through,

just, maybe,
     it will say, "Enough,"
on behalf of the poor;
     it will say, "Enough,"
on behalf of the suffering;
     it will say, "Enough,"
on behalf of the broken;
     it will say, "Enough,"
on behalf of the aged;
     it will say, "Enough,"
on behalf of
     the disenfranchised,
          discounted
               and dismissed,
on behalf of
     the voiceless,
          the mourning,
               and those left behind;
     it will say, "Enough."
On behalf of our God,
     Who says, "Enough,"
     let it be **"Enough!"**

Whose Side Are You on?

We all choose   *-cides*:

sui	-cide
homo	-cide
geno	-cide
infanti	-cide
aborti	-cide
feti	-cide
matri	-cide
patri	-cide
sorori	-cide
fratri	-cide
parri	-cide
uxori	-cide
regi	-cide
tyranni	-cide
omni	-cide

We all choose   *-cides*:

one way
or
another

Whose side are you on?
Who and What do you support?
(Who and What support you?!)

We all choose   *-cides*:

one way
or
another

We   make   a   choice:

sometimes hard…
sometimes easy…
always costly…
never free…

Whose side are you on?

We all choose   *-cides*

Would You Do It for Me?

Smoke everywhere in this three-story apartment
in North Hollywood—3 Alarm Fire, there in minutes
Firemen, paramedics, ambulances
on the scene in minutes
spraying hoses, smashing windows,
wrapping folks in blankets,
going back for Fifi and Fluffy

Would you do it for me?

Ray-Ray's house burnt to the ground
in my part of town over several hours
Lost his mother and his brother
and one of his babies
he couldn't get back to
when the gas stove blew

Lock down at San Juan Capistrano High
Police there en masse in minutes
with blueprints and plans
to get everyone out to notified
parents at a Starbucks evacuation site

Would you do it for me?

Police were already there in Uvalde,
waiting, just waiting outside
at our Brown sisters' kids' elementary
while the shooter shot and shot and shot,
killing babies and teachers
We need first responders
not after-the-fact preachers

Touted coast to coast all over news media
after the San Bernadino Inland Regional Center massacre
left fourteen dead and twenty-four injured,
were the heroic officer's words
as he evacuated survivors,
"I'll take a bullet before you, that's for damned sure."

Would you do it for me?

In my neighborhood and many others like it,
police shot
an elderly grandmother
in her own kitchen through her own open blinds
while she pounded a tough cut of meat to make dinner;

another mother screamed, mourning her mentally handicapped son
killed before her eyes in their own backyard
after she called police for assistance
during one of his mental health meltdowns;

another child, an eight year old, sent out to play in the park
with a green and yellow water gun in the summer
was struck down as an "armed threat"
and was picked up mid-day by the coroner before his mother arrived;

another brother, coming out of his own apartment,
never made it back to family inside
when a police woman on the wrong floor
thought it her floor and her apartment;

another wife and mother filmed her husband, executed
before her children's eyes in their car
as he attempted to pass his license
taken from his phone wallet
through the rolled down window;

another wife, pleading with officers not to shoot up her garage
with her husband and infant inside, prayed,
if only they'd acted out their curse-laced threats
and killed her, too;

another homeless man "succumbed,"
tasered, then battered beyond consciousness—
all captured on hospital surveillance

and the cop cam (*"audio only"*);

another and
another and
another and

another day,
another "police incident"

ALL SHOT.
ALL UNARMED.
ALL MAX MELANIN.
ALL DEAD.

You do the right thing for some,
but would you do it for me?

Index of Titles

About the Author

Photograph by Elsie Dixon

Sr. Betty A. Harbison, a native North Carolinian who grew up in Los Angeles, California, retired in 2021 from a thirty-eight year secondary teaching career with diverse urban, socio-economically challenged student populations. Seven months later, she put that lifetime love and expertise to good use and began serving as the Education Specialist at a homeless and battered women's shelter in Los Angeles. In working with students and adults at the site, she often chuckles and fondly describes it as " 'the little red school house on steroids' because I never know whom I will see, what ages they may be, what they may need, how long I will have to work with them, or if they will still be there the next time I return." She sees herself dominantly as a resource for academic support to assist parents in working with their students and navigating the educational systems, and perhaps a bit more as a teacher determined to instill into/ indoctrinate anyone and everyone she encounters to be "life-long lovers of learning" and confident proponents of his/her own abilities to excel once the individual "learns how s/he learns" "to study smarter not harder," the latter she touts as her original adage probably pilfered by a former student or parent now in advertising. Many of her students have competed and been published in national and international contests and publications, such as, Poetry Out Loud National Recitation Competition, Creative Communication National Poetry Contest, Celebrating Art National Art Competition, American Library of Poetry National Competition, the Los Angeles Times, and Poetry in Time of Crisis: An International Chinese Poetry Symposium (during the Covid Pandemic Shutdown) and have garnered national medals and regional recognition in Scholastic Art and Writing Awards and local city-wide competitions. Thriving on what she terms, "the pursuit of excellence— our only goal," she loves working with students to prepare their works for competition or performance and delights in exposing them to other experts and professionals who can help them in honing their craft. During her first two years working at the shelter, over fifteen students have won publication rights in national competitions, including one third grader selected as a "Top Ten Poet" in her age group nationally. "I have had my high school club members graduate from everywhere, including Harvard, Princeton and Yale Universities." With a twinkle in her eye, she continues, "I tell all my other students, "You finish the set. All I am missing are a Cambridge and an Oxford graduate. You do it, and I can die happy." Although it may be difficult to get her to talk about herself rather than "her babies," she is a proud graduate of the University of Southern California with a B.A. in English and M.S.Ed. in Education, credentialed to teach K-12/Adult and has a Gifted and Talented Education Certification, as well as English Language Learner Certification. She has taken classes at Cambridge University, Cambridge, UK, California State University, Los Angeles, University of California, Irvine, El Camino College and spent her freshman year matriculating at her mother's alma mater, HBCU Bennett College for Women in Greensboro, North Carolina. She is a singer, writer, painter, who loves dogs, holiday and holy days celebrations, being part of national organizations devoted to social and cultural advancement, such as Delta Sigma Theta Sorority, Inc. (Life Member), the National Association of Negro Musicians, Inc. (Life Member), the National Black Sisters Conference, and the National Educators Association/ California Teachers Association—Retired/ Montebello Teachers Association. High on her list of favorites is visiting new places and experiencing others' cultural traditions…as long as she has access to corn flakes occasionally and milk daily. Currently, she is a newly professed Catholic Religious with the Sisters of Social Service in Los Angeles.

Publishers Note

Daxson Publishing was created to help marginalized artists and their allies publish their work, so the world can hear their voice. The vision for this publishing house is to help people get their work out there, and not have them struggle finding their way through the publishing process. Everyone's voice deserves to be heard, and we are here to help. If you are interested in submitting a manuscript, email daxsonpublishing@gmail.com. Support our cause by buying books from daxsonpublishing. com.